FLYING OFF THE SHELVES

THE

FOOD ENTREPRENEUR'S

GUIDE TO SELLING

Tessa Stuart

Published by Stamford Brook Press

Copyright © 2015 Tessa Stuart

ISBN: 978-0-9576028-1-6

Tessa Stuart

Dedication

To James, who has put up with my tweeting for far too long, and to Flora and Sukey – for being unfailingly supportive. Thank you.

Contents

Who I am and why I wrote this book

I've run focus groups for twenty years. That's a long time to spend with eight strangers in a living room talking on a topic, for 90 minutes, six or twelve times a week, year in, year out.

I researched Cadbury's Wispa bar with chocolate lovers who went on strike and stopped speaking when not given chocolate.

I've worked out just how much of the mysterious Milk Tray man's body needed to be shown, climbing through windows, in expensive 80's TV ads.

I've talked to mums about innocent drinks' kids drink – and to a roomful of lively, funny, bouncy eight-year-old kids – when the product was just a little white wedged-shaped tetra created for the research by innocent drinks' new products team.

When I started my career, clients had big market research budgets and the time to run a lot of research projects. They believed that you marketed to passive consumers who passively received carefully chosen marketing messages. They thought customers would receive and believe anything clients chose to tell them, just like blotting paper.

The clients sat behind a one-way mirror in the suburban focus group facility, drinking crappy, massively over-priced Chardonnay, and peering at and commenting on the eight people in the group, as if they were monkeys at the zoo.

After yet another night finishing work at 10 pm in Wolverhampton and wearily bedding down in another anonymous Premier Inn, I had a revelation.

> "There has to be a better way to understand folk and their actions and beliefs, one that involves them alongside me and the packaging, and is more real-life."

I knew I could have real, live, funny, illuminating conversations with folk scooting through their shopping in the way that we all actually do – distracted, in a hurry, hurling stuff into our basket in five minutes, not really thinking that hard about what we're buying.

Quick, candid conversations could be held right by the shelves, not inaccurate reconstructed views to please the researcher (and the client watching behind the mirror), justifying the £40 incentive shoppers would receive at the end of the research session, as they went off into the Croydon or Swindon night.

I wanted to peek into people's trolleys to see how they balance health and convenience when they shop, to have them point out for me their actual shopping choices from the shelves. Not recall it for me in a faux-memory-reconstruction in a hot stuffy sitting room in Caterham, alongside eight total strangers....

So began my apprenticeship in the aisles, working with clients such as innocent drinks and Firefly Tonics who really needed to understand how their pack messages were working at the point of choice, on the supermarket shelves.

Shoppers don't hang out in the chilled aisle for long, it's just too cold. I layered up, and stayed there for five hours at a time, watching what caught people's eyes, checking out their body language, asking "what?" and "how?" questions that worked brilliantly for clients. It felt real, interesting, proper and useful.

So I pushed it further. A test for a new product, mocked-up, for innocent drinks, there on the shelf – did people notice it, pick it up, *want* it?

They did. The pack mock-ups flew into trolleys. (I had to run after folk heading to the till to explain why the packs couldn't be bought! We had made just six of them in the innocent kitchen that morning.)

I had brilliant, short, sharp, focused conversations with very helpful, intelligent shoppers. We're all marketing-and-media literate now, so everyone can deconstruct packaging messages on the spot.

Body language and eye movements don't lie.

When shoppers touched the product, (innocent's stipulation, to see if the pack was working **all by itself** to get noticed) I would scoot over from my spot lurking at the end of the aisle, by the discounted cheesecakes, and ask my three key questions. Folk were really interested to be part of a quick process about what they chose to buy.

They'd show me, pointing it out, what worked for them and what didn't, how it felt to touch, look, hold the pack, what they knew about the brand, the ingredients, the price, the size, the competition – all the aspects that came together in their decision whether to reach for that product.

Talk to 40–50 people this way, and you can map a whole audience for a product. On to that you can map all the "trigger points" that bring folk to a brand.

Then you can really understand how your pack and pricing and ingredients messages are coming across from that store shelf. This helps you sell more. Small businesses are the engine of a revived economy, and run by the hardest working people I know; to me, it's a huge privilege and a joy to be part of their success.

So I got to do my kind of research 9 am–5 pm, without spending yet another night in a grim Travelodge in Wolverhampton, or treating people like an alien species of (distancing research terminology) "respondents".

It felt like a win-win.

I became obsessed with refining this approach.

I used it for different categories of food, from yogurt to soup, muesli to crispbreads (warmer categories to work in than the chilled aisle!), in café-restaurants such as Leon, Itsu, and Daylesford, to look at queuing flow at peak times, menu development, atmosphere, staff welcome, for artisan brands such as hand-made chocolates and Swedish crispbread, for world food brand unearthed in Waitrose…

I am now a total evangelist for this *new way* of understanding how one little pack can talk to consumers, on the shelves, where new competitors appear all the time and competition is fierce, and the losers get de-listed, and lose their coveted spot on the supermarket shelves.

I like "arming" challenger brands with their insight ammunition against the multinational food corporations.

This book, *Flying Off the Shelves*, is your set of sales tips.

It's not a "workbook". (Why does that sound like a Dickensian punishment?)

It's a tips book. One to pick up, browse, to give you some inspiration, some little tasty *practical* ideas *and* the feeling that you can do them.

It's a book for you to read about other entrepreneurs' insights, and to inspire you to have your own "aha!" moments.

Who is this book for?

Flying Off The Shelves is for all those entrepreneurs with a quality food or drink business big idea, and limited marketing budgets and time.

What this book will do for you

Do you have a unique and fabulous food business already off the ground?

Are you looking for tips on selling into stockists faster and better?

Do you want to ensure that loyal customers buy your product again and again?

Then this book is for you. Read on!

If you're at an earlier stage and you are planning your packaging and branding for your new food product, café, or even app, then you should take a peek at my other book, *Packed*, first.

Packed: The Food Entrepreneur's Guide – How To Get Noticed And How To Be Loved, is available on Amazon.co.uk and Amazon.com and on Kindle.

It has tips from successful food and drink businesses such as innocent drinks, Muddy Boots Foods, MOMA!, Graze, G'Nosh, Peppersmith, Jimmy's Iced Coffee, Rude Health and Higgidy.

These are all businesses with real food products, but many of the tips and hints these founders share are just as applicable to "virtual" food tech ventures too.

So whether you are:

- setting up an artisan food delivery company
- a vegan supper club business online
- opening a porridge-only café in Shoreditch
- seeking an Ocado listing for your Indian meal kit
- launching smoothies in the Wirral

Packed has inspiration and advice for you.

If you want cracking ideas on:

- identifying your niche
- testing your market
- the right pack sizing
- clever packaging

I've also included interviews with owners of independent food stores, so you can read up on their likes and dislikes when being pitched to.

Section 2 has my A-Z of *Flying Off The Shelves* tips – tried and tested techniques for getting your products noticed, nudging customers, building customer loyalty, and getting inside your customers' heads, so you understand how to sell to their secret desires…

Section 1: Buyers Being your best in front of buyers

Tips from the experts: a food business stocked by Fortnum and Mason: Pistachio Rose, Indian fusion bakery

(NB: All these tips for independent stores work just as well for when you are approaching supermarkets later on.)

Rekha Mehr, who got her **Pistachio Rose Indian fusion bakery** products listed in Fortnum and Mason, and who has worked in buying at Waitrose and Amazon, has this advice.

Approaching buyers: initial approach

1. If you're struggling to find the name of a particular buyer, try looking through the trade press, as buyers are often asked to write about/comment on category trends. LinkedIn can also be another way to find buyers' names.

2. Avoid making contact on Mondays (certainly the mornings), which are typically spent preparing for internal trading meetings.

3. Send a brief email, which takes no longer than 60 seconds to read, and communicates what problem your product is solving and why it's right for their customers.

4. If you're struggling to get a response from the buyer, try other members of the team such as the assistant buyer, or buyer's admin assistant, who can advise you on a better time or way to get in touch, or who may be able to move things forward themselves.

5. Remember that you're trying to build a relationship, so every point of contact counts.

Unrequited communication is still visible, so always be polite!

Pitching it right

Rekha's tips for when you get in front of the buyer are:

1. To earn the buyer's trust, demonstrate that you understand the market that your product sits in, because after all, it's their category on the line.

2. A unique selling point (USP) is the key reason that customers purchase, so be sure to highlight it to your buyer, whether your product is cheaper, better value, or the first of its kind.

3. Don't be tempted to bad-mouth competitor products, as it will weaken your argument. Instead, focus on the things that your product does best. Let the facts speak for themselves.

4. Be prepared to talk about pricing. You don't have to agree a final price there and then but you must be able to present a sensible offer.

5. A helpful framework to work to in your thinking is opportunity: market behaviours, problem: gap in the market, solution: your product!

Tips from the experts: making your first approach to an independent store owner

Let's start with the independent café-deli. This is likely to be your first port of call when you are starting out.

To be chosen and stocked, you obviously need to consider how to approach them in the best possible way, not put their backs up, and present your product effectively.

Maike Hachfeld, an independent store owner, runs **café-deli Hack & Veldt in Chiswick**, London W4. She is constantly contacted by new food businesses asking her to stock them.

She shared her pet annoyances with me, and her ideal preferences for exactly how food businesses should approach her:

"OK, here's the first thing that bugs me....

Instead of the details I need about the margin, they give me recommended retail price only.

I run a London deli, and I set my prices myself, so I immediately get a little annoyed. I begin to think: "You are telling me how to run my business, and that's a bit cheeky...."

I need to know:

- What is the unit cost to me?
- What is the minimum order?
- Is it via a distributor I already use or a new one?

- What are the delivery dates?
- If I order by noon, can I get it next day?
- What are the payment terms?

I like:

- to get a sample of the product to taste
- a contact name and the email
- hard copy of these contacts – it is good to have.

What matters to me most of all?

It's the taste, above everything else. If I like it, I will consider stocking it. If not, I won't.

What annoys me?

If I go back to the company, and say I am interested, and then a week goes by, and nothing happens – so if you are on it, please be on it!

After 24 hours, things fall off my interest radar, and I won't follow up, because my brain is full of new things.

What's my major pet hate?

Please, please don't turn up at the start of business, at 8 am, when there is a massive coffee queue.

Don't be that very irritating, totally unannounced person demanding to speak to me about his or her products.

Don't ever lie to my staff, and tell them you have made an appointment to see me, when you haven't.

Don't ever drop in a case of your drinks, saying to my staff: "Maike ordered it", when I haven't done any such thing.

Think about exactly when you should offer me a taste of your product. Because if you want me to taste a curry sauce at 9 in **the** morning, it's not going to happen!

Don't constantly chase me with sales calls. I will deal with it. It's so counter-productive when people call me the next day and the next day and the next day...."

Tips from the experts: Marcus Carter of Artisan Food Club

Marcus Carter of Food Ventures and Artisan Food Club, who is very experienced at selling new artisan producers into independent stores in London and elsewhere, has this advice to share:

"Remember you're selling profit to the shopkeeper, not the food. You **must** know your margins, the wholesale price, credit terms and order numbers. So many new producers come to me, focused only on the food they make...."

Tips from the experts: Ben O'Brien, founder of Sourced Market, St Pancras Station and Old Street Station

Here's another perspective from Ben O'Brien, founder of Sourced Market at St Pancras Station, London, on how you should think about approaching Sourced.

Says Ben: "For you to be listed, you need to offer me *better quality and value* than what is already on my shelves – so, a pie that tastes better, and costs me less than the one I am stocking.

If it's a product we don't sell, is there a *demonstrable demand* for this product?

Do a case study with a retailer before you come to Sourced to prove there is demand for your product.

Presentation and packaging are really important as "people buy with their eyes."

Have you done the "four metre standing back test" – is it clear what your product is? Our Sourced Market customers are in a hurry to catch their trains with limited time – are you doing enough to catch their eye?

Can you merchandise for Sourced in a bold and colourful way? That might get you space with us. We don't have enough time to do it.

Are you committed to independents? Sourced does not stock what is in the supermarkets.

Don't just drop off samples. Leave a feedback form with us, get feedback, and if it's good, that might get you a meeting.

Include your delivery charge so we at Sourced can clearly calculate our margin.

If you've met us at a trade show, always, always follow up.

Tips from the experts: Selfridges

Leah Anderson-O'Loughlin, is former bakery and dairy buyer at Selfridges. Her role for nearly two years until March 2015 was to source and develop the best possible brands and products for the bakery and chilled goods categories in Selfridges' food halls. She was accountable for growing sales and profit and delivering a product offer at the forefront of London's buzzing food scene. Here's her advice:

The introduction

Avoid sending an introductory email or calling a buying office for the first time on a Monday. Mondays are a buyer's busiest, and often most stressful day; usually spent doing lots of reporting and attending internal trade meetings. An email received on a Monday runs the risk of being buried under a deluge of others that flow in that day, and potentially forgotten.

Email rather than call. Email allows you to give the buyer key information to decide if your product is a fit for their business.

Your email should include a summary of what your product is, the brand "story", and why your product will sell from the shelves of the store you're pitching to.

Always include a proposed cost and retail. Don't be shy about including any awards, accolades or impressive market stats about your product too.

If you can, use your personal network to have someone introduce you to a buyer. A warm introduction works wonders in any industry, so don't be shy about asking.

Embrace social media, especially Twitter and Instagram.

Buyers, particularly those that work in a trend-driven business such as Selfridges, will often browse social media to uncover exciting new products and concepts before they hit the mainstream, and to get updates on existing trends.

Set up a social media presence from day one; it's free and gives you the opportunity for dialogue with buyers, customers and fellow entrepreneurs.

Social media is an invaluable tool for small brands that can't afford traditional PR and advertising methods.

The conversation

Be confident. A buyer definitely won't believe in your product if you show any uncertainty.

Key traits buyers are looking for in new suppliers are passion and knowledge. Passion for the success of their brand and product, and the knowledge to ensure the product is a long-term success.

Demonstrate your familiarity with the business you are pitching to, where you see your product and why, how prices compare to elsewhere, supply limitations, and be prepared to negotiate, even in that first meeting.

Know every detail about your product and brand. If you haven't got a particular answer, let them know you'll follow up on email later. Just make sure you do follow up!

Most buyers are working on a "one-in, one-out" rule, for every new product listed – another needs to be delisted to make space. You need to convince the buyer that your product is better and more commercial than their current offer, or adds something they don't currently offer.

Listen to the buyer's feedback on what could be improved about the product, branding and packaging. Whether you agree with them or not, it's a buyer's job to know what works in their stores, and what their customers are looking for. Be flexible and use their suggestions and criticisms constructively. Be open to making small changes not just to secure the listing, but also to optimise sales in the long run.

The long term

If you're successful in gaining a listing, the next challenge is in ensuring your product remains on the shelf long-term.

Buyers are accountable for the ongoing sales of the ranges they buy, so it's paramount to do everything you can to maximise sales. This can be via promotion, product tastings, in store events, online campaigns… the list goes on!

Once your product is listed, your buyer becomes your brand's representative internally: develop a good rapport with them to ensure you're always front of their mind for exciting opportunities for increased exposure and sales. A collaborative relationship is crucial to long-term success, so focus on good communication, willingness to participate in events or promotions, and continuous innovation.

The obvious

Don't promise anything you can't deliver: Make sure any deal you agree is 100% sustainable for your business.

Research food safety standards, and ensure you either have the required certifications, or are able to arrange them easily. Some stores will help with the cost of this, but not many. A buyer simply can't pursue a product that doesn't adhere to food hygiene standards, policies and procedures.

Tips from the experts: on approaching Whole Foods Market

Sarah Hilleary of b-tempted, a gluten-free food business shares her top five tips on approaching Whole Foods Market and selling there:

Whole Foods Market launched my gluten free brand, b-tempted, in 2009, and they remain one of my favourite customers.

My method of getting listed was to walk into the store and have a chat with the person behind the bakery counter.

All I wanted was the name of the bakery buyer, but I must have made an impression because he made a telephone call and the buyer came straight down!

Luckily I had some samples with me (actually intended for a friend's office), which I gave him to try.

There was a clear gap for a gluten-free bakery brand at that time, and I was listed within two weeks. While things have changed since then, some of the principles remain the same.

Be passionate! Build the relationship with the buyer and be realistic.

The number one thing that comes across to a buyer is your passion.

Be confident and respectful when making your approach.

If you know an existing producer, ask them to make an introduction if it is appropriate and they are comfortable in doing so.

Be aware that buyers have timelines that they work to, and also have a lot on their plate. So if you do not get an immediate response, gently follow up but do not harass!

Be realistic with your timeframes – be aware that once a buyer says yes, it can take at least one month to get through all of the paperwork for a listing.

Where do you sit in-store? What is your price point?

Is there a gap for your product? Which category or aisle will you sit in? Bakery, grocery, prepared foods? Know where you will sit on the shelf, how you are different from each of their existing brands, and how you will add value to their existing offering.

What is your price point? Make sure that you include a sufficient margin for yourself and any distribution margin if you are using a distributor.

Have a retail-ready product

This means having a product that is ready to be sold. The buyers, while they are often passionate foodies, are not there to get validation from or to bounce ideas off. While there may be some variation in the final specification of your product, it is expected that you will know how your product will look and be packaged.

Get your labelling, barcodes, ingredient and allergens declarations completed.

Know your case sizes, shelf life, trade prices, and payment terms. Prepare your technical specifications (or find someone qualified to do this).

If your packaging is not ready, at least create physical mock-ups.

What is most important is that they *taste* your amazing products!

Know your story, supply chain and distribution

What's your story? From where do you source your ingredients? Do you source free range and/or organic ingredients? Are there any health benefits?

Whole Foods shoppers love wholesome products that are carefully sourced and produced and they love hearing the story behind the producer.

What is the lead-time of having your product produced?

How will you get your product into the stores?

Is it ambient, chilled or frozen?

Will you use a distributor or deliver directly?

If you are delivering direct, Whole Foods Market has a centralised distribution centre in Hertfordshire. Make sure that you factor in the cost and time of delivering there, and think of this when negotiating your lead time and minimum order size.

Using a distributor is worth considering. While at first it may sound as if they take a lot of margin, it may be worth it if you intend to use them for other trade customers as they will take responsibility for your invoicing, payment collections and deliveries, leaving you to focus on business development, manufacturing and marketing.

In-store sampling and marketing

Once you're in, it is super-important that you do as much as possible to help your product fly off their shelves.

The number one way to build your customer base is by getting samples of your products into the mouths of consumers!

Whole Foods Market shoppers *love* meeting producers face to face, once again it is your passion and story that people love.

Build that face-to-face relationship with your consumers and enjoy doing it.

Make sure that you create a marketing programme of visiting each store a few times in the first few months of launch, and then commit to an on-going in-store sampling campaign. Whole Foods are also very active on social media – especially Twitter and Facebook, so get involved!

Of course, not everyone who approaches Whole Foods Market will be listed. If they say "yes" to you, congratulations!

If it's a no – don't fret – regroup, take on board their feedback and improve your product. Look for other sales channels with a view to approaching Whole Foods Market again in the future.

Buyers change, and so will their objectives. A no can simply mean "Not right now".

Hazel Wright's Eat Toast Dunk Me Marshmallows are stocked in Whole Foods Market (and Selfridges). She advises:

These buyer guys are busy, with huge jobs, so pick your moment to interact. Monday mornings are a no-no, as they need quiet time to prepare a weekly report. Avoid Mondays at all costs!

Find out HOW your buyer wants to communicate; they are all different, whether text, email, mobile, landline.

Whenever you do make contact, be clear on exactly what you need out of the contact, and communicate this clearly and succinctly. Keep it light, bright and short.

Offering regular samplings to your buyer keeps you and your product front of mind when the shelf re-organisation happens!

Offer new products regularly – deliver what you say you will.

Tips from the experts: supplying through local sourcing from Tesco's local sourcing buyer

Sarah Mackie, Tesco's local sourcing buyer for the UK, explains how you can use being a **local** producer to your (commercial) advantage:

We have scouted local suppliers who were selling on stalls in shopping centres. Orkney Smoked Cheese started out in Tesco Orkney's shop, and is now stocked throughout Scotland.

How can you approach Tesco? And what will you need to demonstrate in that buyer meeting?

Sarah's tips list:

1. Write to local store managers.

2. Look out for meet-the-buyer events.

3. Come to us with a barcode.

4. Know your market.

5. Show us you will market locally and sample your product in our stores.

6. Know your commercials [these are the details Sarah Hilleary listed that buyers need about your margin, distribution, shelf-life].

7. Have good, robust packaging, that'll survive and get noticed on shelf.

8. Be technically savvy, and "safe" (get your product tested for nutritional data).

9. Have a good "reason to buy" for the customer in the aisles.

Tips from the experts: how to present to a buyer from a brand new food business, Claudi & Fin

Lucy Woodhouse is co-founder of Claudi & Fin, whose Greek style frozen yoghurt lolly multipacks are available in 300 Sainsbury's stores. Here she talks about the approach she and her co-founder Meriel successfully made to Sainsbury's.

Know your market

You can never know too much about your market place. Live it and breathe it as a consumer. Walk the aisles. Taste all your competitors' products.

Benchmark your price, your USP (unique selling point: your point of difference from the competition), your ingredients, everything.

Visit the British Library for access to free market data and then conduct some of your own research if you don't have the answers. It is vital to show your buyer you understand your market and where it's going in the future.

Know your customer

Do they need your product? Understand exactly why they do, and make sure the buyer knows too.

Does your product address a particular issue for consumers? In our case, we couldn't find a lolly that we really wanted to give to our little ones. Our response was to make our own delicious lollies, using great tasting, all-natural, quality ingredients, so we wouldn't feel guilty.

Know your supermarket

What does your buyer want? What is their business trying to achieve?

We felt very strongly that we should be answering as many of the buyers' requirements as possible from both a category and an overall business perspective.

We studied Sainsbury's 20/20 Sustainability Plan and built it into our pitch, explaining how our product addressed certain issues.

It showed we understood the supermarket's key business requirements and how our product could deliver on some of them.

Brand, brand, brand!

When supermarkets are driving own-label development and sales more than ever before, it's vital that your brand really stands out (Sainsbury's own-label makes up 51% of their overall sales).

You need to be able to build a loyal customer base, who want your product more than any other, especially when the supermarket does an own-label version much cheaper.

Whether it's through making the consumer feel better about buying your product, or through characters, your brand has got to work on the inside (ingredients) and deliver on the pack as well.

Branding is what will carry you through. Show your buyer amazing branding and packaging that will make them see "pound signs".

PowerPoint presentations

Lucy emphasises:

I love hearing people talk passionately about something they believe in. I don't want to look at a screen with bullet pointed information, I want to watch the presenter come alive and tell me why I should believe too.

We wanted the Sainsbury's team to remember our product, fall in love with the characters on the front of the pack and most of all feel as if they couldn't possibly do without it on their shelves. So we didn't use a computer. Instead, we printed massive A1 and A0 posters of our front of pack to look like iconic film posters, and we talked to them about why we were so excited about our product.

Persuading buyers that they need you

1. Be clear when you meet your supermarket buyer **exactly** how you are going to grow his or her bottom line income in the category he or she manages.

2. Are you persuading shoppers to "trade up" and spend more for your "better, more premium" product?

3. Are you bringing shoppers back into a category that they have left through boredom and lack of excitement?

4. Are you bringing in shoppers who don't normally shop in that supermarket?

Remember, with the discounters and online nibbling away at supermarket sales, and customers buying smaller baskets of food when they shop, growth sales figures for the supermarket buyers' targets have to come from:

- more sales
- persuading customers to pay more for more "premium" products, and a higher margin for the supermarket on each product sold
- both.

We won't go into all the charges that some supermarkets make to their suppliers for being on the shelves at all, but that was/is another source of income for the grocery chains.

Amelia Harvey, Head Cow at yoghurt challenger brand **The Collective**, formerly head of sales at Gu Puds and before that at L'Oréal, says it's important to be aware what's pre-occupying a typical supermarket buyer's head as he or she manages their category:

- sales figures
- profit
- new launches
- promotions
- wastage costs (of products that don't fly off the shelf and have to be destroyed).

They have a lot to think about, and uppermost is the need to hit their category targets.

Products that sit in new categories excite buyers. If yours is a new product in a new category, that's a reason why they would see you. If you are a premium product from which they could earn more margin on each sale, that's even more of a reason.

So keep an eye on "tired and dull" food categories – could your product energise an old or create a new category?

Examples of new categories are:

- birch water
- bircher muesli.

Examples of a new packaging format revitalising a category is peanut butter in 30 gram pouches, launched by Pip & Nut into Selfridges.

The buyer has a lot to think about, let alone where their own career is going, and how their organisation is doing, before listening to your pitch.

Tips from the experts: building relationships with supermarket buyers

Amelia Harvey Of The Collective:

1. Don't farm out your sales to anyone else. Only you and your close team can have that absolute passion and drive to move your business forward at pace.

2. Make sure the buyers get to see the whites of your eyes; go and see them, don't hide behind phone calls and emails.

3. Manners – you never know where someone will pop up again!

4. Belief and persistence – there are extreme highs and lows, you have to find ways to manage the lows and get yourself up and fighting again.

5. Responsiveness – the faster you can turn around a response from a buyer or consumer the better!

6. Be easy to do business with – don't make long and complicated proposals, buyers just don't have time to wade through them, especially if you're a small business.

7. Never stop selling!

Amelia says: "I take coupons around in my bag with me so if I meet someone who hasn't tried our yoghurt, I give them some, and if I'm in front of the yoghurt fixture in store I'll do some selling right there and then!"

(For more on how these coupons work, Coupons, page 55.)

Tips from the experts: Henrietta Morrison, founder of Lily's Kitchen, organic pet food, stocked in independent stores and Waitrose

Lily's Kitchen operates in an extremely competitive environment. Mars and Nestlé, massive companies, sell 90% of pet food in grocery stores. If you are in a similar situation, don't let this put you off.

By producing superb quality products, which are made with passion and dedication, you can cut through the domination of the big guys and speak to consumers who share your values.

And the best thing is that as a small company we can be really nimble and produce new products quickly – we don't need to go through tons of committees and approvals, which can take bigger companies years rather than weeks.

We are really lucky to have been in the position of store buyers calling us rather than us having to hound them for an appointment. It's ideal when it happens this way as it makes the negotiation slightly easier.

I wish I had realised that year one is the honeymoon period, and that, even if you do brilliantly, the second year of negotiation can be really tough.

I think I must be the most inexperienced food producer to ever launch in a supermarket! I had little idea of all the ways groceries can charge you for a listing – it is endless – everything from funding the promotions, to paying for the listing to paying gate fees (the fee that you are asked to pay when you go on promotion), there can be overriders (and all sorts.

This is when you've delivered an outstanding year of trading and occupying the first, second and fourth sales slot!

I dread to think what it must be like for brands struggling further down the list.

So do remember to build all this into your margin so you can fund some of the activities and still be able to have a profitable business.

You can also say no to many things – the supermarket will make demands for a long list of marketing activities but you do not have to agree to them!

Henrietta's seven sales secrets for sales in supermarkets

1. Make sure your product looks fantastic on shelf. We always take newly designed packs to the supermarket to ensure they stand out on shelf. What looks great in the design studio may not work at all in a crowded supermarket environment.

2. Do engage with the buyer by sending in samples of your products and inviting them to attend your stand at a trade fair.

3. Be open to comments and feedback – buyers are experts in what will work and what won't.

4. Think about launching exclusively with one supermarket chain – the upside is that you can cut your teeth and learn the ropes as well as building a strong relationship with the buying team.

A time-bound exclusive deal will also reap rewards, as the store buyer is much more likely to "hero" your brand, and you need every little bit of help in the early days.

5. Invest in data. Nobody likes paying large sums of money for data, but it is really helpful to buy a snapshot of your category, so that you can say how your competitors are doing and plan what your likely rate of sale will be.

6. Have a really healthy new product development pipeline – buyers love seeing new ideas, and new products can mean more shelf space, which will help you get noticed more.

7. If you see that one of your products is trailing in terms of sales, make sure you have a number of solutions when you meet up with the buyer.

Time is rarely a healer on the grocery shelves – if it's not selling then there's an issue with the product, or most likely, the communication on pack.

Tips from the experts: Jim Cregan, co-founder of Jimmy's Iced Coffee

Jim Cregan founded his company with his sister Sooze after he found delicious iced coffee in Australia and wondered why there was none in the UK. His four-ingredient iced coffee is now stocked in Selfridges, Ocado, Whole Foods, Waitrose, Tesco Express, Nisa, BP and Welcome Break.

- Don't send an account manager, you (the owner) need to go.

- Build a real relationship.

- Be honest about what you are up to, where you're going and how you're going to get your rate of sale up in their stores.

- Don't go exporting because "international" sounds fun, as you'll be taking your eye off the real ball.

- Make their life easy by doing your homework.

- Don't be afraid to challenge them. They need to know you're strong, and business is a two-way street.

Tips from the experts: Tom Mercer, founder of MOMA! Foods.

1. You have to have serious tenacity in trying to get hold of buyers – call 10 times a day if you have to – but only leave a message once, that way you don't piss them off!

2. Be clear and concise about the *key* top line elements of what you are pitching.

3. But also have a more comprehensive pitch – how you can support the launch with sampling, marketing initiatives, what promos you plan to run, etc.

4. Be passionate! Despite all the rational arguments, buyers will be swayed by sheer enthusiasm – it can be infectious.

5. Get to know your buyer – what they like and what annoys them – so you make yourself an easy supplier for them to deal with.

Section 2
A–Z of sales tips
customer psychology insights,
Mailchimp magic and much more

Aiming to be bought on automatic pilot

You've created a new food product, and you are hoping for big things from it.

What **essential** journey do you need your new customers to take?

This is the path that you need to encourage them to travel over time:

Awareness ------> Interest-------> Action -------> Buying on "Automatic Pilot".

Your product must:

- get attention on the shelf (whether that's an online or a physical shelf)

- create interest

- create desire

- stimulate action – and get bought.

And it must do this over and over again.

Just as you form fond memories of a close friend over time, the brain's neural pathways are built by pleasurable sensations with a food product, repeated over time.

Check out all the little toddlers in their Bugaboos, in the supermarket or on the street, clutching their innocent kids' smoothie. Aged two, these kids are definitely able to identify "their" product on the shelf in the supermarket and ask for it, without words!

These very young kids have made the connection between a pack on the supermarket shelf and a pleasurable sensation of taste and comfort. They've spotted the colours, the taste and the shape of the item they like.

(This is why the clever founder of Ella's Kitchen, Paul Lindley, put his children's food products not in jars, but in brightly coloured, child-friendly, coloured, squeezy pouches; he'd worked at Nickelodeon in children's TV, and he knew that something children could hold themselves would help out parents, and that kids would love the sensation of holding "their" food.)

How do we lay down product memories in our brains?

Brand connections are laid down over a long period of time, and are so sub-conscious that we are hardly aware of them with our rational mind.

Think about your own favourite chocolate bar, or savoury snack, or cereal. Or the yoghurt you buy weekly. You probably don't ever think about the process of buying these things very consciously.

The sight of them on the shelf brings to your subconscious mind, pleasurably, all the occasions when you have eaten it before, and reinforces why you should buy it again – *now*.

Out your hand goes, to pluck it off the shelf, and put it in your shopping basket. You've barely even thought about it consciously.

The cognitive short cuts we ALL use...

In our daily lives, we all use habits, routines of behaviour that are repeated regularly and occur sub-consciously, which simplify our lives.

Otherwise, we'd never get round the supermarket in a reasonable number of hours. If we were weighing up all the possible options in the yoghurt aisle or in cereals, we'd be there for days.

In the supermarket, we all use these cognitive short cuts to help us navigate the huge range of choices.

The "cues" of where it is in the supermarket, the colour, the pack size and shape, the logos, are held in your brain to help you make the choice swiftly again.

Think of Kellogg's cornflakes' cockerel on the packet – I bet you could actually pick that out in the aisle, even with your eyes half-shut, because your brain is so familiar with its cues.

Switch and hold

To get a customer to switch from what they have been buying to buying your product, and to reinforce that new habit so that they continue to buy from you, is the tricky task that all new food products have to achieve.

This "history" with you is what you have to encourage your customer to start building all over again with your new product.

You have to **disrupt and change** their previous behaviour.

You must do all you can to encourage a new habit to form and to be maintained. No "backsliding" to the previous familiar product!

Otherwise they may try you once. But they'll revert to their familiar choice when they next see it.

Your main weapon is **taste levers** – to be so memorable on the customer's palate, that they have enough of a recall of your flavour, that when they see you again, they remember that you were very good the first time…

But you can also use your **packaging** to "cue" positive associations – with the right use of ingredients, words, and images.

You need to help the shopper understand how to use your product – especially if it's unfamiliar, and give them lots of ways to use it – so that they finish up that pickle or smoked chilli paste and then buy another one.

If you're sitting in the top shelf of the fridge at the back or in a cupboard, you're out of sight and out of mind. Your selling job doesn't finish when customers have bought your product.

You need to do everything you can to embed that product in their brain, so that it becomes the "automatic choice" the next time they see your product.

This takes time.

But to get valuable customers who buy you repeatedly with little or no prompting, *is* your Holy Grail. So everything you do in marketing and selling needs to work towards that goal....

Grabbing those customers and not letting them go!

Amazon

Amazon is a 24/7 global shop window for your non-perishable food products.

This is how:

- go to Seller Central
- £25 a month to use
- ship to Amazon's warehouse
- see and manage all your inventory online.

Fergus Chamberlain, founder of Gran Luchito smoked chilli products, including paste, mayonnaise, oil, ketchup, now stocked in Tesco, Marks & Spencer world foods, and Whole Foods Market, explains why he made it a priority for his Gran Luchito smoked chillies range to be on Amazon early on.

Being on Amazon gives you, from Day 1, the chance to have a national listing. I send stock to Amazon's warehouse in Swansea and they pay me every two weeks. I wake up and find orders have happened overnight, and they're all fulfilled by Amazon.

Being part of Amazon's Add-on programme means my products can be added onto existing orders, and with 1-Click ordering, buyers have total security of purchase.

I really recommend it for sales of your products.

Boldness

It took me two years of stalking **innocent drinks** before I hit upon a way to work with them. I offered them my kids – as children to taste their prototype drink, in response to a request on their website. They emailed back that they had plenty of kids (from the local school).

Me: "Kids can be wild, do you need me to come and help with them in the sessions?"

innocent: "No, we're fine, thanks."

Me: (later) "How did it go with the kids?"

innocent: "It was... a little wild!"

Me: "Well, I am very local, have kids, work with kids, work in food research, have worked with kids in food research..."

innocent: "We're fine, thank you, we can manage by ourselves."

A week later....In-box ping!

From innocent drinks: "Here's your chance – a research project brief for the kids' drink..."

Me: "Lovely, thank you very much!" (punching the air, singing, dancing)

I share this to show that sometimes the *only* way to get the thing you most want is to keep at it, be creative, and to get lucky.

Convenience stores

According to Richard Hyman, a retail consultant, quoted in the *Telegraph* in February 2015:

> "Online is about 6% of the grocery market, and convenience is much bigger. Online is a sexy topic that everyone wants to talk about - it is presented as the greatest disrupter we have ever seen in retail.

> But the convenience store and its growth has been a bigger disrupter.

> It has encouraged a change in shopping habits. It is enormous.

> It has encouraged people to fragment their shopping."

Hyman's argument is that by opening convenience stores on high streets and next to stations, the big four supermarkets have encouraged Britain to shop little and often for groceries, rather than buy lots of food in one weekly shop and potentially waste some of it.

This high visibility of convenience stores on our high streets has also prompted shoppers to buy food from the new breed of independent food retailers, the butchers, the bakers, the independent coffee shops and the café-delis, as well as their Sainsbury's Local or Tesco Metro.

This Sunday morning, I watched an urban professional with his young child in a buggy head straight into Grind, an artisan coffee shop in Putney, and buy a cappuccino for himself, and croissants to take home to his wife for breakfast.

Itsu's half-price sale attracts young professionals working late to swing into the stores and buy sushi for dinner, because it's half-price. They don't want to go to Sainsbury's and buy the stuff to make sushi from scratch and anyway, it would cost them more money.

There have never before been so many places to buy food on the high street as today. And this trend to convenience on the part of the shopper presents you with a huge opportunity to:

- get in front of them in lots of independent/convenience stores/cafés (see Independent Stores, page 73)

- offer them convenient options in your products – soup/drinks/snacks/ "to go"

- think "short-cuts" – sauces, dressings, chutneys, seed mixes, all help the time-pressed savvy shopper seek out simple solutions.

Coupons

Valassis enables you to have manufacturer-issued coupons that you can use outside the supermarket store promotions you may have agreed, on full-price items, so that you can encourage new customers to try your brand, with less cost and risk to them. Worth considering, once you are stocked in a supermarket.

www.valassis.co.uk

Call 01536 445251 to find out more.

Each time you raise a new coupon you pay, but once you have got the print costs and initial fees out of the way, you just pay a small handling charge.

Sampling in-store combined with offering coupons to customers who sample, really helps persuade them to buy on the spot.

Customers

Your customer is your friend's sister who likes eating a big tub of yoghurt with her girlfriends when they are catching up on chat.

Your biggest fan is the person who quietly buys your chocolate every week and shares it with her friends.

We're in a "sharing" economy now, which is not just about Airbnb or Uber, but a world where a Twitter follower of yours will happily share on her Instagram feed a photo of your gluten-free cakes in Whole Foods. Your customers are your sales force now.

(For a good example of how to Instagram oats excitingly look at Rude Health's recipe photos.)

We're herd animals. We are unconsciously influenced all the time by what people do around us. So do all you can to influence your customers.

How do you find customers?

Start talking about your food business to absolutely everyone not just your family and friends. They know you already. Talk to strangers.

Find a way to get yourself and your product in front of the strangers who will become your customers:

• Share a market stall with a friend.

- Be part of a healthy eating event.

- Give a talk, anywhere you can find an audience.

- Do you have a small local business networking group? Offer to talk or make cakes/offer your gin at one of their evening networking events for free.

- Take free food samples along for folk to taste, and a discount card for your services as a trial offer if you cook/have a delivery app.

- Make cards to hand out with your details on (and the offer).

- If you're a baker, talk at your local Women's Institute event.

- School fairs are great for start-ups, low cost, and a really good way to practise your patter (ring the school secretary of your local primary school for details of dates and be prepared to give a small percentage of your takings to the PTA).

- Run a supper club, and get your friends to promote it to their friends.

Rude Health started selling their first muesli, made at their kitchen table, at markets. Now they sell in supermarkets.

You need to get some customers, keep them, get more, keep them, repeat repeat, repeat.

I heard **Paul Lindley, founder of Ella's Kitchen**, explaining how to increase your customers:

1. Get more customers.

2. Get existing customers to buy more from you.

3. Get more products launched and out there, to bring new customers in.

4. Go to more countries, export.

5. Be more efficient (pay your suppliers later, hold just enough stock).

6. Mergers and acquisitions.

Design that gets you noticed

Dan Shrimpton is co-founder of Peppersmith (classy mints and gum, check them out in Boots now and lots of other places).

> "If we hadn't had really good packaging, we wouldn't have got off the ground.
>
> The packaging made us different, fresh, premium, natural, *all* at first glance.
>
> When you are starting out, your packaging *is* your communication, you don't have budget for anything else. It's crucial."

Peppersmith used a brilliant design agency called B & B Studio, whose design handwriting is all over lots of lovely brands, including innocent drinks, Pip & Nut, and Bear.

Desires

What are your secret desires? Who are you *really* in your head? We all have desires. And so do your customers.

The advertising industry's dirty little secret is that they always "sell to desires".

That desire is the "better version" of ourselves we carry in our heads that we *all* promise ourselves we'll become "one day" – cleverer, thinner, fitter. (But secretly want easy short cuts to reach.)

Here's exactly how you can manipulate those desires.

What does your customer hope to be:

- thinner?

- healthier?

- more beautiful?

- smarter?

Here's how – when you are in a store, offering tastes of your soups, casually drop into your explanation to prospective customers that they are "only 127 calories, but so filling and very tasty, with the anti-oxidants broccoli and kale".

Your listener will register some of this.

If she's a woman looking to be thinner, she'll be mentally nodding her head, and saying to herself:

> "Mmm, useful to know, that's low in calories, now, let's see how they taste, and I'm trying to kick bread, so maybe this soup is all I need..."

If you are selling protein dynabytes, little filling bars of deliciousness, as Rosie Millen, Ms Nutritionist is, you might choose to place your protein bars in gym/yoga/wellness cafés, where folk have worked out, feel (momentarily) wonderfully lithe and strong, but are a bit snackish after their yoga/Soulcycle:

> "I've worked out, so I am thinner/stronger/fitter, and a little treat can't hurt – I deserve it...."

Can you work your product into the story that your customer is telling herself?

Distribution

How does this help sales?

Your first posh London stores are likely to be one of the following:

Fortnum and Mason

Selfridges

Harvey Nicols

Daylesford

Fortnum and Mason is inundated with tourists buying tea, or basically anything with the Fortnum and Mason label on it.

Daylesford is ladies who lunch (lightly).

These places are therefore superior "shop windows" for your product.

The data on sales in these places, gets your foot in the door to the next buyer – at Ocado or Waitrose, Sainsbury's or Tesco, Budgens or the Co-op groups.

It's up to you to sample your socks off, and make your products fly out. That way, you earn the right to be stocked somewhere more mainstream – in a bigger shop window.

And don't neglect your independent stores. These are convenient for your (well-heeled) customers and they are likely to be loyal to you, as long as you sell a reasonable number of products.

Although the rate of sale of your products per week may be lower, you won't face the six months to a year timetable to hit sales targets that Waitrose, Tesco or Ocado will impose on you.

Do something consistently every day

Whatever you do, do it regularly.

If you tweet sporadically, people won't see your tweets. The research shows that folk spend on average about 15 minutes on Twitter in any one session, but not longer.

Tweeting first thing is good. It's when most food businesses wake up and head onto Twitter.

It's also when they are looking for interesting/funny/topical/health-related content to re-tweet. Your tweets could be that material…

For more detail on this, and top tips on scheduling social media posts and tweets, see Social Media on page 110.

Encouragement

Build a supportive gang of other food entrepreneurs for moral support when the mountains to climb seem far too high.

They can be in a different category of product to yours, but perhaps a complementary one. So buddy up with a maker of crackers, or a crisp brand, if you are a dip producer.

You can be each other's wingman, inspiration and support and person to let off steam with, when your immediate family and friends are bored with your business obsession. You can brainstorm together, get creative on problems and come away supported and with new thoughts for your own enterprise.

If you are in complementary fields, such as cheese and biscuits, or tortilla chips and dips, then you can run competitions and make offers to each other's customer lists, and grow your own customers by getting them to sign up to your newsletters.

You **need** friends like this in your corner. If you are a solopreneur, *you* are the one creating the energy every day that powers your business along. You won't have an endless supply.

Food business friends are your "charging zones" where you get the confidence, support and inspiration to keep on keeping on.

Energy

Always smile and say hello. This sounds so obvious, but positive levels of energy beaming outwards from your market stall, your exhibition stand or your sampling on Saturday in store, will draw people to you.

If you look tired or boring, so will your products!

Enthuse the staff in the delis or shops where you are stocked. Give them what you make to try.

A friend of mine, Amelia Rope, sells her chocolate in Liberty London's chocolate shop. All the staff there have great enthusiasm for her chocolate and are keen to talk about it with customers! That creates a mini-sales force on your side to sell your products for you!

Event catering

This is basically like sampling, but at an event where you think the people attending a) could afford to buy you b) might be interested enough to do so c) are the right audience for your product.

If you make marshmallows or cold press coffee, make a batch and get them in front of an audience with money. (Escape the City runs London events for City employees who want to start their own entrepreneurial projects, and who come along to events to hear about other folk's jumps into the unknown. You could be there, either sharing your story, or your products, or both with an interested captive audience.)

You might wince at the cost of this, but innocent drinks donated tonnes of their smoothies, and if your product is at the end of its shelf life, but with a few days to expiry, then it's better than wasting them. Innocent built a reputation for generously donating to every school fair or event in their local area (and getting in front of the mums and kids who were their prime customer group).

Approach women's magazines such as *Red* magazine, and offer free healthy delights for their goodie bags at events. Offer goodies for an event for a new chic organic farmshop or entrepreneurial event (Enterprise Nation, Start Up Britain, Virgin Start Up, BIPC at the British Library run lots) and hand them out there and then – with a big smile!

At Food Start Up London in Shoreditch, devised and run by Victoria Albrecht, the guys doing the catering were a founder of a food delivery app, which allowed the audience to really experience the food, to try it before they bought through the app, to meet the company's staff, and to get a sense of the company's ethos and values. Not a bad way to get in front of a hundred hungry people who might then buy your product…

Fear of missing out

Also known as scarcity.

We all hate the idea we might be missing out. You can use this to your advantage for your limited edition product, which might be seasonal, or too expensive to offer outside December, but which sells well then, by describing it as "available for a limited time only".

Amazon constantly shows you there are only "4 CDS/books in stock", and what do you do? You buy. They are nudging you to do so. (See Nudges, page 88).

Fun

One of my favourite brands, Jimmy's Iced Coffee, brings energy, fun and friendliness to everything they do.

Jim Cregan, the founder, announces their new stockists on YouTube videos. His "we're stocked in Boots" announcement is hilarious. Have a look. As is his latest: "Hey London"; I defy you not to want to drive to the beach drinking iced coffee after seeing that one.

Make your brand fun to hang out with.

As Mr Chase, founder of Tyrrells Crisps, told us in the audience at *The Grocer's* Build A Brand conference, "your brand should aim to be like the really interesting person you meet at a party".

Not the drunk tedious over-exuberant person banging on about themselves, but the amusing friendly one you want to see again.

Jim Cregan regularly speaks at the *Guardian* master classes and elsewhere on how he started out.

He raps. He plays rock, paper, scissors with the audience, as his warm-up trick, and the winner gets a Jimmy's Iced Coffee beach towel. He's the best guy at warming up a room I've ever seen.

Guild Of Fine Food's Great Taste Awards

The Guild Of Fine Food runs the judging process for awards. I really recommend you enter your products. (February each year.)

It's a robust judging process, where all the products are tasted blind, out of their packaging, by panels of expert judges, who don't get paid, but give their judgement and time because they believe in the scheme. Judges are chefs, deli owners, buyers, food writers, cooks and specialist food retailers such as artisan bakers and butchers.

For a product to win a star, it gets passed in front of a lot of very good palates. Foods are judged on technical criteria – is it cooked properly? – and on taste.

The judges will give you useful feedback on what to improve in your product to win a two star.

If you win a two star it can be the fast track to getting stocked by independent stores, as they often rely on a Great Taste Award as a signifier of quality.

The Great Taste awards logo and the star ratings are recognised by independent store shoppers, as a mark of quality – helpful to your new product.

So don't delay, enter. It's worth it.

Habits: the ones that help you get bought

Think of how you like your tea – with milk? Any sugar? I bet that you are as irritatingly specific about how you like it as I am – "more milk please, yes, a drop more, more than that, yes, a bit more, just a bit more... great, thanks."

How soggy do you like your cornflakes? Can the milk be on them for only a *certain* amount of time? Do you eat muesli with yoghurt and blueberries, and NEVER with milk? Will you eat granola, dry, in handfuls, out of the packet, whilst on the sofa watching TV in the evening?

This is the level of detail that I find out when I stand in the aisle and ask people about breakfast habits for cereal and yoghurt clients.

So why *do* I ask all these questions?

If you, as a food company, *don't* know how customers are using your yoghurt or your muesli, then you have absolutely *no* idea how to encourage them to do it more and, therefore, to get them to buy your product more often.

Frequently people eat your product in ways you **absolutely** don't expect.

Innocent didn't realise that adults were drinking their kids' drink, because they liked its thinner texture.

People take and use your product in the way that fits *their* individual lifestyles. It helps if you know how they do that, then you can acknowledge those habits in point-of-sale material in stores (recipes), or neck tags on your bottle or stickers on your pack, and explain how customers are already using your product to new shoppers considering buying.

Gran Luchito smoked chill paste and oils offer recipe cards in their newsletters and feature a new recipe and enticing photos each month. Images like that might just drive their existing customers to dig out the paste from the fridge and make a meal using their products…

My clients chase new customers. That is, of course, crucial for a new challenger brand to do.

But it's so important to get the customers *you already have* into the habit of buying and using you regularly.

A customer's lifetime value to you is major, if they buy you every week. So *always* think about how you can reward and encourage the people who do buy to remember you, and not wander off to their previous brand.

Here's how Higgidy do it: they publish poems sent in by Higgidy pie customers on their website, and they send customers Higgidy aprons as a thank-you.

I'm sure you have a coffee habit. Whitbread, who owns Costa Coffee, must be rejoicing as we order buckets of milky lattes in Buckingham, Beckenham and Bridgenorth. (Note: it's quite possible these aren't *genuine* Costa locations, I just enjoy alliteration.)

When people are out and about breakfasting, they are looking for the familiar and the comforting. Who hasn't stood on a grim, cold, station platform in the dark waiting to get onto a train with horrible or actual *missing* food options? Yes, Virgin Trains, I am looking at you....

That's when travellers can easily form a habit of buying something familiar, hot and almost instant, and not just coffee!

They will be delighted to see you, a brand they know, available on a station platform.

MOMA! porridge bought there, or from Sourced Market in St Pancras, a gorgeous place, which also does Monmouth Coffee, has improved my very early morning train journey to Sheffield for work projects.

Less fashionable places, such as station platform caterers (AMT), and trains (Great Western, Virgin) are locations where passengers are spending a lot of very tedious time early in the cold grey dawn, hungry, with their wallets to hand, and feeling the need to treat themselves a little. These are where your brand should be, as Cuckoo bircher muesli is.

Where the available alternatives are grim (Crewe station comes to mind), a good quality food brand can do very nicely.

That's why Cuckoo Foods' bircher muesli will also do well on Great Western Trains, where early-morning customers are captive, bored, keen to snack, journeys are long, and the on-board food offer is limited.

So think about whether the habit you need to succeed and get sales can be encouraged elsewhere by you popping up in front of your customer....

"I'll have what she's having...."

Remember the famous scene in Katz's Deli from the Hollywood romcom *When Harry Met Sally*? When Sally has a very good time in a crowded restaurant and a nearby customer says:

"I'll have what she's having..." (Look it up on YouTube.)

We are herd animals, and all of us are influenced by what others do. That's basically what Twitter is built on – curiosity about other people. Ditto Facebook.

I bet you've been in a restaurant and caught sight of another diner's order heading towards their table and thought to yourself: "That looks better than what I was thinking of, I'll change…"

You can use this desire that we all have to copy what other people do to get folk interested in stocking you.

Drop a note to a prospective buyer about where else you are stocked, to create interest. (For more on this, see Innovation and Trade shows, page 76.)

You'll find that the buzz of a sampling table will bring folk over to look and to buy. Other shoppers will see a crowd, and come over.

Independent stores

There are now **a quarter more** independent food shops in the UK than there were a year ago, with bakeries and fishmongers increasing, and a 65% rise in independent delis and grocers, 20% of these new stores are in London.

So what are you waiting for?

You can take your ketchup to a butcher, and your marshmallows to a deli, or an independent coffee shop.

Marcus Carter at Artisan Food Club knows many of these independent stores and is a useful man to know to get your product into these places. (Find him in the acknowledgements at the back of the book.)

But there's another reason why, for food producers, independent stores are often a much better place to be than the supermarket.

The entirely different mindset of the customer

When you enter your local deli or fishmonger or butcher, you're not thinking about price. If you were, you'd have driven to the supermarket.

You're there because they have high quality interesting new speciality foods, and they are convenient.

For the independent deli/food store customer, it's all about convenience, browsing and considering what will taste great that Friday evening, or what you are treating your guests to.

The same goes for your local fishmonger. And the same goes for weekend farmers' markets.

The minute you step inside your independent food store, the seduction begins. The environment is entirely different from the supermarket.

It's more personal, more real, the produce is there, looking fresh and delicious, the senses are assailed by smells of cheese, perhaps an enticing display of cakes too, or some stunning fresh fish laid out, and you're already, in your head, planning a number of meal menus. You're open to trying new things and to looking at new brands. You are, in that moment, a food connoisseur, and your senses are heightened.

In the supermarket, where I interview customers, the experience is functional and routine. Not much sensuousness there, unless you are near the in-store bakery.

Because every aisle has deal stickers – "buy one get one free", "two for £5", and promotional flyers hang overhead, customers become much more price aware.

They can look at the price of a product and immediately check to see if there is a similar one in the store's own-label nearby.

It's so much harder to do that in an independent store.

People shop fast in supermarkets; in independents, they slow down and browse. The service at the deli/coffee counter means they wait in line and have time to look around and take in products – and maybe add them on impulse before they get to the till.

Innovation

Tips from the experts: Adam Sopher, co-founder of Jo and Seph's Popcorn

Innovate!

Create a "world first" if you can – or at least a UK first.

In our case our alcoholic popcorn range, including our Gin & Tonic popcorn, made with 5% real gin, brought something completely new to the snacks category. It has helped create fantastic headlines such as "Popcorn that gets you drunk", and developed our brand yet further.

Twitter research

You can send the right journalists your products to taste as opposed to a mass send out to everyone. An incredible number of people will have on their Twitter bio a comment such as "Gin lover" or "Lover of all things peanut butter". Send the right journalist the right product for them and they will love you forever.

Trade shows

We had no contacts in the food industry at all when we started, so trade shows have been critical for us to meet the right buyers.

One bit of advice I've learned over the last few years... when following up with buyers after the show, don't chase them...it doesn't work!

Far better to *update* the buyer on what new stockists you have, new flavours, great new PR, etc.

Food festivals, also known as consumer shows

These shows are tiring to do...really tiring...but an amazing way to get a lot of feedback (positive and negative) really quickly!

You're also bound to meet a celeb or two and so shows are a great way to get some influential people on your side!

Piggyback on bigger brands

We've never had much of a budget for anything at Joe & Seph's, so partnering with bigger brands has been a great way for us to benefit from their marketing muscle with minimal cost to us.

Bigger brands love working with small, new brands, so personalising your packaging or product for them, could be worthwhile, if they will help get your name out there."

I worked with **Lucy Thomas of Tastemaker Ltd** when she was at innocent drinks for eight years as their chief "taste bud" developing smoothies and veg pots. Lucy has also worked at Unilever and Le Cordon Bleu, with Graze.com, Rebel Kitchen, G'Nosh, Plenish Cleanse, and is a Ballymaloe trained chef.

Her tips for gaining new customers through innovation are to:

- find an unmet consumer need
- invest in relevant food and ingredient trend research
- taste good

- challenge industry assumptions without neglecting food safety responsibilities

- choose your packaging format and size carefully.

To reduce risk of cannibalisation (i.e. your new product stealing sales from your existing products), there are levers in new product development that you can use to your advantage:

- colour e.g. innocent's green smoothie stood out in a sea of berry and tropical coloured drinks

- flavour profile e.g. a spicy dip may be bought in addition to a creamy dip but customers are less likely to buy two creamy dips together

- ingredients to target different occasions e.g. oats for breakfast snacks, high protein for gym snacks etc.

- appeal to different people e.g. kids, older people, food allergy sufferers

- launch into a new category that is relevant to your brand e.g. Rebel Kitchen has plans to follow their mylk drinks with a launch into healthy snacks

- think about the different moods of your consumers

- seasonal/limited edition rotating line to add variety without adding an overwhelming amount of choice.

Remember sometimes it is better to improve what you have rather than launch more products in the same range.

Editing choice can increase sales as consumers feel less overwhelmed at the fixture and therefore more likely to buy.

Jump start locations

Getting your product into somewhere prestigious such as Selfridges, Daylesford, or Fortnum and Mason, or a swanky hotel group such as Starwood or aboard an airline, such as Virgin Atlantic gives you profile.

Associating your new brand with these elegant, aspirational, environments helps your brand acquire these qualities by association.

The fridge mini-bars of hotel chains can be a great place to be stocked. The hotel guest has already committed to paying for the room, and a rummage in the mini-bar is all part of the experience. They aren't thinking: "I'll pop out to my Sainsbury's Local for bargain crisps." They're thinking: "Let's be naughty, and open the wine, and eat the snacks…"

The in-flight eating options on airlines are another great place to be – for visibility. After all, the passenger will be staring at your packet on their tray-table for quite a while before it gets removed….

Kick-start your business heart

You can kick-start your business by entering supermarket competitions where you pitch your product and they list you in stores for a year.

Claudi & Fin did this and went into 300 Sainsbury's stores.

See founder Lucy Woodhouse's tips in the Buyers section (see page 34)

You could pitch to the Dragons in the Den, as Harriot Pleydell-Bouverie, founder of Mallow & Marsh did.

Doing *Dragons' Den* gives you great publicity and creates very useful customer awareness. Harriot turned those Dragons down, and found investment elsewhere.

Winning Ocado's Next Top Supplier 2014 competition was the springboard for Hannah Rhodes of Hiver Beers to get new stockists, including Ocado, who read her story in the press.

Kickstarter

I'm not covering crowdfunding here, but besides raising funds and building a band of supporters, it allows you to make a lot of noise around your product. It works for restaurants looking to fund another branch and helps products to get to prototype. A successful campaign on Crowdcube such as Camden Town Brewery's £1,639,270 for 2.18% equity offered, shows that their beer drinkers are more than prepared to put their money where their mouth is.

Labels

Hanging about in supermarkets as I do, I often spend time between interviews tidying the clients' products on the supermarket shelves and showing them off to their best advantage.

I turn the labels to face the front, I check the shelf stackers have not put products on the shelves upside down, I pull forward the products at the back of the shelves. I present them so they look impressive, attractive and inviting to potential customers.

Customers respond to a tidy, well-stocked, assertive display. It makes your brand look confident. It makes them more likely to buy your product.

Lonely, single products from unknown brands are the ones left on the supermarket shelf. The more unloved your products look, the less attractive they are to shoppers.

The fewer of them that sell, the less inclined the supermarket store manager is to re-order.

Automatic stock re-ordering systems adjust to the lower rate of sale...

It's a vicious circle.

In an ideal retail world, and one with attentive staff that is owner-managed, such as an independent deli, your products will look neat.

In a supermarket where the shelf-stackers are spotty teenagers busy discussing *World of Warcraft*, they're not focused on the job that they are doing at the pace of a snail. They don't care.

The solution?

Bribe your friends to make sure you look neat on their local supermarket shelf. They'll help you out, and if you've made a tribe of them on Facebook, they might even report back to you whether your new product is actually on the shelf in the stores – because it may well not be. Friends can be your eyes and ears on the ground.

In an ideal retail world, and one with an attentive staff that is owner-managed, such as an independent café-deli, all of this may happen – your product may be nicely lined up on the shelf, looking smart and enticingly ready for sale.

As for making your products stand out in independents, Brew Tea has some helpful suggestions (see page 102).

Lifetime value

It costs you time and money to make a sale.

You'll be pitching and convincing folk to buy you, during long mornings spent smiling and sampling in a Budgens, a Piccadilly Whole Foods Market, Waitrose, a Broadway Market stall, Kerb, Taste of London, the BBC Good Food Show, Abergavenny Food Festival, Kew Gardens events, RHS shows, the list goes on....

Appearing at Meet The Maker events in Selfridges, at health "workshops" in swanky gyms such as Equinox, or at Google HQ events, gets you up close and personal in front of your potential customers.

It feels endless and exhausting, putting yourself out there constantly. But, it gives you *real* human contact with your customers.

There is **absolutely no substitute** for the founder of a food brand showing up and selling in person. I've stood alongside the founder of G'nosh, Charlotte Knight, in John Lewis food hall as she samples, and seen the impact on the customer of meeting the founder.

Amelia Rope has built a devoted following with her samplings in Liberty's Chocolate Shop. I've watched her engaging vividly with each new potential customer one to one. Amelia is really passionate about her values and product, and allowing customers to try her bars gets them over the hurdle of not knowing the product, and makes it easier for them to buy from her.

If you are groaning about these costs of your time as a founder, think about the "the lifetime value" of each customer.

My food clients find that sampling product and meeting customers **consistently over a period of time** in the same store leads to an uplift in sales. The rate of sale increases and stays high for several weeks afterwards.

Once they have started to buy your product, if you can get them into the routine of buying you once a week, that's a sale that keeps on happening and bringing you income. (See Habits, page 69.)

Establishing these connections really matters. Their lifetime value to you is major if they buy you every week.

Limited editions

Limited runs allow you to:

- test your idea for good sales and possible inclusion in your main range

- introduce seasonal ranges (good if you make iced coffee and need a funky flavour to create sales and interest in the chillier winter season)

- organise meetings with buyers to show your innovation credentials and forward thinking

- build your products' presence and space on the shelves

- attract more customers with a specific ingredient or nut-free/gluten-free option

- have a reason to contact journalists/bloggers with something new and exciting (see Amelia Rope's tips on pitching to journalists, page 92)

The downside is:

- additional packaging and NPD costs

- risk of failure

- risk that your new product takes sales from your existing products.

How to minimise risk?

If you have a mailing list, try the potential idea out on your subscribers. Do the same on Facebook.

Look for gaps – what's not currently available? Can you make it?

Can you make it better than the existing options (and still make money from it – often the graveyard of "better" but more expensive for your customer ideas)?

Luck

Fergus Chamberlain, Founder of Gran Luchito, explains how he got lucky:

> "The thing about luck is you can create it. I'm lucky that people like my Mexican smoked chillies product.
>
> I simply sent our product out, saying: 'This is from Mexico.'
>
> *Jamie Oliver* magazine phoned up, and we ended up with a half page of editorial in the magazine.
>
> Lulu Grimes, *Delicious* magazine editor, said it was 'the nicest thing we tried last year.'

Big companies spend millions of pounds on creating products that they hope people will like. You can get lucky as a small producer simply by making something that works for people's tastebuds."

Mailchimp

Building your own database of customers is really important. Mailchimp allows you to do this free.

You're crazy not to use it. Here's why.

Showing up in people's inboxes is a really intimate way of reaching them, and nudging them to think about you.

Tweets are ephemeral, and can be missed. Everyone checks email.

Right from the off, innocent drinks built "the innocent family", their own big database of customers, which they could use for research with simple Survey Monkey questionnaires.

They thanked their "family" with a gift each Christmas. My bright orange (juice) innocent socks have finally, sadly, worn out, and the mini spruce tree they sent me is now a fully fledged tree in my dad's garden.

Innocent also, sensibly, asked signers-up to specify their age, gender, and number of children at the outset, so they could use parts of their database to test different new product ideas.

Mailchimp gives people a sense of who you are, beyond having just your product on a shelf.

You can use Mailchimp email newsletters free (until you hit a certain number of subscribers), to:

- thank your customers

- remind them to buy again from you

- research new product ideas

- ask them to come and support you at events

- help fund your project on Kickstarter to buy a van (as Claire at Summer House Drinks did, very successfully).

Nudges

We all need nudges. Such as...

"Have you put the rubbish out?"

"Did you lock the door?"

"Have you sent a birthday card to your mum?"

"Have you done your tax return?"

HMRC's campaign this year, featuring a beatific dentist smiling away having completed his tax return on Shepherds Bush bus stop ads, gave me a nasty nudge of recognition and guilt when I saw it.

How much more, then, does someone new to your product need a nudge? The answer is "a lot". (See Powerful promotions, page 93, for more on this in a store context.)

You need to gently nudge prospective customers towards a desired goal.

Nudge marketing is all about gentle suggestions that require little effort from the audience, maybe a competition of Like and Share on Facebook, or a peek at your cool photo of cake on Instagram.

It can be something as simple as signing up for a newsletter.

Nudging your potential customer directly from awareness to consideration to purchase in a single journey is a huge ask.

Though it can be done when you sample in store – if you get good at it.

Think of all your opportunities to nudge being a learning process in which you and your customers learn more about each another, and they travel closer to buying you.

Ways to nudge folk include social media of all kinds, Mailchimp newsletters, press coverage, blogs, pop-up events, giving talks (on nutrition or your start-up journey) and sampling.

A nudge is any inventive way of getting in front of your current or potential customers and can also be a promotion on the shelf. (See Powerful promotions, page 94)

Objectives

It's easy to run around being a busy fool when you start out, convincing yourself you're doing well.

Setting big scary objectives and making sure you meet them is how you move the business on to the next level – and more sales!

Tips from the experts on setting objectives: Dan Shrimpton, co-founder of Peppersmith

Dan told me that reflecting should be one of the most crucial activities in your business. He shares how Peppersmith considers what's working and what's not, and how they alter course accordingly.

"If you don't reflect on what you've done, how do you know which bits worked and why they did? And what to do next?

Learn to focus. If you try to focus on all customers, you haven't got the resource as a small company. It's easy to get over-excited and spread yourself too thin.

Try and re-evaluate everything.

Is this still the right customer?

What is actually working?

Set objectives on Monday mornings. What are the three big things to do that week?

Here's an example. I spent some time in Whole Foods Market, sampling. We all did, at the beginning. I was meeting maybe 50 or so customers.

Then I realised that my time was better served by working out how to get us on an airline, where our products would be in front of two million people, as we are on Virgin Atlantic. It took a long time, but we did it, which is great for visibility.

It's easy to rush off to every show in the summer, and work all your weekends as well as the weeks. But it's utterly knackering. You repeat the same sentences over and over, and that can mean you just get jaded and exhausted.

Evaluate which shows are worth your time.

What's the cost of each encounter with a potential customer in staff time, and which shows achieved the objectives you set for being there?

We feel that being at Taste in London is high profile, so we do that. We are now more picky about what other shows we do."

Oblivious and Obligation

There you are, products arrayed enticingly on your sampling table or your stall, a smile on your face.

Nobody is making eye contact. They're in their own worlds. Ignoring you. It feels very awkward.

You want to reach for your phone to feel connected to someone, to make that feeling go away. Put the phone away. Look up and out.

My day job is interviewing passing shoppers in the supermarket aisles. I'm the weird woman lurking by the yoghurts/soups/cheese biscuits/innocent veg pots.

Here are my five tips on connecting with total strangers:

1. Notice something about them.

2. Say: "You look very...[fill in your complimentary adjective of choice here, but make it something you've noticed about them, what they are wearing, or their shopping] …ready to try"/"the discerning kind of person who...." (offer your product).

3. Don't ask closed questions to which the answer is no. "Do you like chilli?" "No."

"No" closes any conversation down.

4. When they taste it, watch their body language. Are they enjoying your product? While they are standing there, mouth full, eating, this is your chance to explain a little more.

5. But gently. Think of two or three trigger words – your ingredients. Because they have stopped, and you have fed them, they are now obliged out of politeness to give you some attention.

I watched this in Waitrose. My food client was offering tasty tapas items at Friday lunchtime. Everyone was receptive. They were hungry. Everyone went to the shelf afterwards and bought.

That's the power of obligation right there.

Patience, you'll need lots

If I had a ten pound note for every food business founder I've met who says: "It takes so long to get stocked anywhere," I'd be so rich I'd be relaxing in the Bahamas on my yacht, not writing this.

Every single start-up I meet, even if they have been trading for five years, bemoans the speed at which things happen.

Impatience is what makes you quit a job and start something up, but now you need a mixture of opportunism, extreme optimism, determination, luck, sheer bloody-mindedness and a large dollop of charm to play the long game of becoming a successful food business.

Press coverage

Tips from the experts: pitching to journalists: Amelia Rope, chocolater

Amelia Rope, chocolatier, has the following advice on gaining press coverage.

- I would recommend a small effective PR company in the early days for product placement. They can be useful terriers at chasing the relevant magazines, newspapers and bloggers.

- Appreciate any mention you receive, thank and keep these writers and journalists and bloggers up to date with any new elements to your story (your products, you, your awards, any nominations).

- Try to keep innovating as much as you can a) to keep press interest, as journalists always like something new b) to keep your customers interested.

- You may find some journals feature you more, and others feature you less. Learn from these signals and adjust your PR strategy accordingly.

- You may also find some features converting to sales and others contributing to your brand/profile awareness, but with not much conversion to sales. Both are good.

Powerful promotions (that don't kill your margin)

You've seen the BOGOFs – bet you've bought them on bog rolls too.

They've come in for a lot of flack, encouraging us to "spend more than we need to", "creating waste", and as a cynical ploy by the supermarkets.

Here's why they are a bad idea. (And then here's a better promotional idea for you.)

BOGOFs encourage customers to **always** expect money off or a deal or two for one. Why would you ever buy full price again, with BOGOFs running?

Do you want to be like my first ever food client, with his supermarket customers deliberately *not* buying between his promotions because "they'll be back on promotion next week?" (His business went into bankruptcy last year.)

No. You don't.

But you need to get people noticing you're there, and buying you close to full price right from the off.

What can you do if your product is new, similar to, and close in price to known brands with greater customer awareness?

You need to use some form of opening promotion to compel customer attention.

Habit and speed make us pick the familiar – the easy and fast.

To your prospective customer, you are the "unknown", and the "what if I don't like it, and I've wasted my money?" risk. Unless, of course, you're an Early Adopter, trying new things all the time out of curiosity.

It's worth targeting EAs like me. Our self-worth is (pathetically, I know) based on sharing new food discoveries with everyone.

Supermarket customers are conditioned, in a Pavlovian manner, to respond to promotional stickers.

That's the legacy of the big four supermarkets battling it out against each other for so many years with price cuts. They've trained their customers to expect money off all the time.

If you're in an independent store, with lovely artisan packaging and a story to tell and you can be there in person, a lot, you may not need an opening promotion.

But it'll help persuade folk new to you to try you wherever you are stocked.

Here are the promotional tricks that sensible food companies (like Higgidy) use:

- £1 off introductory offer (or whatever sum suits your product, margins, and seems enticing to customers) when you are launching.

- A "2 for £5 offer", across two different flavours in your range. This can help to shift the one that sells slightly less well, or has unfamiliar ingredients. If you can sell one item to a customer, you can sell them two.

- Combine this with FOMO (See Fear of missing out, page 67).

We've all bought on Amazon when it says "two left in stock". Same principle.

It works particularly well on market stalls, and online.

Combine it with Limited editions (see page 84) and you have even more chance of sales.

Questions

Here are five essential questions for every food business:

1. "Who is buying my product?" Mums with kids? Fitness fans? The over-fifties? Single men?

2. "Why are they buying it?" "Great to have in my handbag or desk drawer if I get faint at work" (cereal bar).

3. "Convenient for before swimming classes for my daughter" (squeezable fruit pouches for kids). "I drive a lot for work and start early" (protein breakfast drink).

4. "Who is **not** buying my product?" Who turns up their nose at it?

5. "What are their "barriers" to trying it? "It's not for me."

NB: this sentence, "it's not for me", is usually **the kiss of death for the product.** When you hear this emphatically announced by your potential customers, as I have in focus groups many times, you know that the lupin seed "innovative" product is not passing muster.

"It's not for me" is frequently used to describe over-priced health drinks, and weird "foreign" foods. Or scary mash-ups such as kombucha shots with kale, or absinthe-flavoured cold brew coffee.

So make sure that your product will work for normal folk in normal places. (And let's face it, London is absolutely *not* normal. I know. I live there.)

Rebranding – risk vs reward

Many food businesses get in touch with me every month and ask me to look at their re-brand designs.

But can tweaking a logo, or changing words into images, magically increase flat-lining sales?

Here are the essential questions to ask yourself *before* you call in a designer and spend money on rebranding you may not need.

WHY are you doing this rebrand?

WHAT is your packaging design currently failing to communicate to potential customers?

WHY are they turning away from you on the shelf to your competitors?

Ask strangers to your brand to look at it on the shelf and tell you if they "get it" straight away.

"It" is the benefit to the customer.

Natural, great taste, gluten-free, luxury, single-origin, are just trigger words on the box, which may or may not be working as intended.

The benefit, the "it", is how using your food product can make them feel happier, healthier or improve their love life.

Here's an actual real-life example from innocent drinks that I worked on in the aisles of Sainsbury's.

Launching a fresh pot noodle would have brought a bunch of new customers into the innocent brand, as a revitalised and improved new product in a very tired category.

Innocent drinks had already spent a year on manufacturing trials and flavour development when innocent's new product development manager came to me with a very specific communications research project in the aisles.

We used mocked-up noodle pot packs we made in innocent's kitchen, the design created by their in-house team, three days of my time in the chilly supermarket in layers of thermals, spying and swooping on shoppers.

Why did innocent drinks, and I, go to these (rather freezing) lengths? Innocent's research brief was super-simple:

- Do people notice the product on shelf?
- Do they touch it?

Innocent drinks stipulated that only when shoppers actually touched it, could I pop out (from behind the stack of Coors beer at the end of the aisle where I was lurking) and accost them with my questions:

"What is it?"

"How would you prepare it?"

"When would you eat it?"

Innocent drinks were insistent that if potential customers could not spot in 15 seconds that:

> "it's a super-convenient fresh healthy veg packed pot noodle that you make in 3 minutes with boiling water any time, from innocent, different from a veg pot"

then the communication on the packaging had failed and needed tweaking.

Customers **loved** it.

They put it straight into their trolleys. Cue awkward scenes as I ran after them and retrieved our mock-up from them, explaining that it was not edible or for sale just yet.

So, is it actually the pricing, sizing, or "benefits for your customer" messages that need looking at, rather than a re-brand? It could be subtle tweaks rather than revolution.

I've worked with big FMCG companies on branding logo evolution. They make very subtle changes, so as not to lose customers.

Customers store in their brains short cuts to finding your product quickly when shopping. They store the colour, the shape, the images of ingredients on pack, the rough outline of your logo, the shelf position, and the spot in a specific aisle.

You may send the stores plans of where your product will be on the shelves. But it's a free for all as far as shelf stackers and store managers are concerned, they can change *all* your best-laid plans for having a great eye-level position.

Brands are often dismayed when I get to the store for research and send them a photo:

"You thought you were on the middle shelf? Well, actually, you're on the top/bottom shelf...."

Stores are **already** hard at work distracting customers from you with their promotional shelf-edge pricing and moving you around. (Marks & Spencer, you need to stop this!)

If you tinker radically with your design, you are fiddling with customers' visual memories of you, which, if you are a new brand, are only just being established.

Are you being stocked in stores that require you to have more robust packaging to withstand shoppers' and shelf-stackers' mishandling? Has your product got less time to get its message across in the aisles? Reasons to consider a re-packaging exercise.

Or is it that you as a founder are bored with the design you started with five years ago? Which is in fact perfectly acceptable to your customers.

Is it your price they don't like?

Is your message about the use of lucuma in your ingredients confusing them?

You aren't going to know how to begin a re-design unless you know what is working and what isn't.

So here are my tips.

- Lurk in the aisles.
- And ask them.
- If you're too busy, I'll do it for you.

(And that's the only pitch from me you'll find in this book. I promise.)

Running before you can walk – why you should slow down

Every entrepreneur I meet is fizzing with new ideas. That's what makes founders start businesses, see niches and go for them, and bring out new products that fly. But, this fantastic ability can also be an Achilles' heel. Why?

Because a lust for "the next new thing" holds you back from the rather duller business of creating and maintaining the initial sales you need to make.

We all know the buzz that comes from new ideas, the chase after the meeting with a new retail buyer, the new opportunity to be on the shelves of a new store.

What we forget is the customers in our first few stores, or Whole Foods or Planet Organic, as we rush to innovate with a new line in a new category.

Your customers, the folk who actually *buy* your drink or soup or bread or cake, need reminding that you are there. You *must* build their habit and keep on building it in the face of competition and copycatting from other competitors.

Every business thinks that its customers know all about what it makes and that they don't need reminding. But we *all* forget.

Until you are the default option, the "always have a cup of tea in the morning", you aren't secure, you aren't an established habit – and it's dangerous for your brand.

Tips from the experts: develop relationships

Aideen Kirby is co-founder of Brew Tea, which is stocked in Waitrose, Harvey Nicols, good independent food stores such as Sourced Market and many other nice spots. (It's a very delicious cuppa indeed.) Here she gives some advice.

Building relationships is one of the best things about being on-shelf with an independent store. You are relying on their merchandising and their sales tactics to get your products sold.

If you work hard to improve sales in a category for them, they will reward you with more shelf space, extra lines and opportunities to do really fun things with them.

If they see you as regularly as possible (even if that is only two or three times a year), especially to sample, you will get to know their staff and customers, get to answer any questions they might have, and find out what weird and wonderful uses people have come up with for your product.

Never underestimate the power of a staff recommendation for your product.

Also get to know your customers – never take for granted that they'll always buy your product, so do as much as you can to keep them interested, be that with fun packaging, social media campaigns, competitions or using them as focus groups to help you improve products (we did this with our chai blend last year).

Be on the radar

While you can generally get in touch with your independent retailers fairly often, you probably can't say the same for your supermarket buyers.

Yet it's still key to stay on the radar with them.

But when buyers get so many emails and questions that tiny companies like us are permanently at the bottom of the priorities list, how can we manage to do that?

The answer is to persist and think as innovatively as possible. If we're struggling to get hold of a customer, we sample at their place, take lots of pictures whilst we're there and then send them a postcard.

It reminds them that we're still interested in them and gives them that last prod – it makes asking for data, help or a favour a tiny bit easier.

Getting back on the shelf

If you look at your rate of sale data and realise that you're selling out in one week then not having a re-order for another three, it's time to get your thinking caps on.

Zero sales weeks that are down to having no stock are your worst nightmare, but not everybody is amazing at managing stock. Sometimes it's because they're too busy or have too many lines to manage, and at other times it's because they don't prioritise your category.

With independents it's easy – you can simply get in touch to remind them to order, or to let them know when you have a promotion coming up, or you can offer to bring some with you to sampling events to ensure healthy stock levels whilst you're there talking to their customers.

With the multiples it's much harder. Sometimes you can get lucky and strike up ordering arrangements, so you can deliver stock outside usual purchase order periods, but this is incredibly rare.

What you then need to do is find any and all ways to get your products back onto the shelf. That might mean contacting your buyer, your stock controller or your favourite store manager, or sending a picture of an empty shelf to head office with a small plea for help, or finding how to move your products out of a monthly re-ordering list onto a fortnightly re-ordering list...

Promotions do help, in that they force orders, but too many promotions do lead to that "Pizza Express" effect (not going there without a voucher!) This one is a toughie, so good luck!

Never forget the real enemy

When you trade in an old or established industry, it can be intimidating, especially if you're trying to do something differently or you're new to it. So it's always worthwhile remembering the cause. For instance, we want people to drink better cups of tea every day by switching to whole leaf tea. If they switch to us or any other whole leaf tea, that's great.

But if a buyer is asking you to dish the dirt on a fellow supplier within the industry whilst at the same time stocking the "same old same old" (for us it's the paper teabag tea), don't be afraid to let them know who the real enemy is. We'd much rather our customers ditched paper teabags all together and used those shelves stocked real tea.

Let your customers know where they can find you

If you have an online store you're using, don't be afraid of cannibalising your sales by letting your customers know where else they can pick up your stuff.

Once you start talking to your customers online, you'll be surprised by how many of them came across you via one of your stockists.

Making it as easy as possible for your customers to pick you up is the best way of becoming less occasional, more habitual.

Sampling

Tips from the experts: Hazel Wright, founder and director of Eat Toast Dunk Me Marshmallows

Hazel took a food science degree and spent 18 years in the corporate food industry before taking the giant leap to pursue her dream of developing her own products and brand – she says: "running my own business is as good as any adrenalin sport!" (Agreed!)

Sampling is an invaluable opportunity to truly engage your consumers and also employees of your retail outlets, turning them into evangelists for your brand.

Sampling is *not* selling, it's an invitation to try with no hint of hard sell.

Fabulous food is about an overall *sensory experience* and using this "lens" you'll really power up your sampling.

Remember your most amazing meal? It wasn't just the taste of the food that made it memorable, it was the table setting, the way the server greeted you, the knowledgeable and enthusiastic description of the menu, how well they answered your dietary and allergen questions, the service time, the presentation of the dish, the aroma and finally the taste.

So here are my top tips to make the sampling a really memorable experience, one that every consumer will want to share with their family and friends:

1. You eat with your eyes.

Make your sampling table look immaculately ordered, clean and inviting. Show your packaging and what the product looks like inside the pack so consumers know what to look for on the shelves later. Keep samples bite size and fresh. Brand yourself with a shirt or apron to complete the picture!

2. Your confidence, passion and knowledge build the confidence to try.

Smile, make good eye contact and invite your consumer to try the product, clearly describing what your product actually is.

People don't want to feel foolish and to have to ask.

In less than ten seconds, describe the key USPs of your product: handmade, Fairtrade sugar, nothing artificial, any benefits.

Invite a taste of your range, "which would you like to try?"

Know your product and be ready to answer any ingredient questions. This is especially important if somebody other than you is doing the sampling – brief them! Make a cheat sheet they can refer to for allergens.

3. Create some sensory theatre

We always use a mini toasting kit that elevates the sampling from a few mallow nibbles on a plate to a real crowd puller.

The dramatic effect of the toasting generates the most awesome aromas of hot chocolate, superb visual display, and builds anticipation to taste the hot gooey deliciousness.

4. Build on those "oohs" and "aaahs" – get a wow

When you get a "wow" comment you know you've created an memorable experience, so reinforce it by commenting, "That's fantastic! What was it you liked so much?" You've just created an evangelist and other neighbouring shoppers will be compelled to try....

5. Create situational reality

Offering some knock-out suggestions of how to use your product in customers' daily lives provokes thought and makes the product really live for consumers beyond a single purchase. For example, "Our Bilberry and Lavender mallow is amazing with Goat's cheese instead of quince jam, try the Rhubarb and Custard mallow swirled into your morning porridge, or on pancakes for a fruity zingy twist, they are great as a gift for a dinner party host instead of flowers that have to be cut and arranged, try our mallows toasted from frozen, it's like Baked Alaska!"

And finally, treat every consumer with as much energy, enthusiasm and focus as you did your first.

Even after six hours of sampling, you're still on stage. Have fun!

Selling at shows

At the beginning, you may find it easier to start at your local school fair, where costs will be really low.

Gill Foreshew, founder of The French Dressing Company, (salad dressing, not Breton clothing!) started by taking stalls at all the school fairs in South-West London, and building awareness of her and her product locally. Years later, her sales in Waitrose in East Sheen are still higher than other stores, because she put all that effort in early on.

Evaluate which shows are really worth paying to be at.

Shows such as Taste London, the BBC Good Food Show and Speciality Fine Foods in September at Olympia, are food showcases and good for profile building, but it's £500 for a weekend stall in the small producers' area at BBC Good Food Show, which means you have to sell a lot of chilli sauce.

Asif, the founder of the Duke of Delhi chocolate bars, told me that being at the BBC Good Food Show is a great way to get your product in front of store buyers, as they all come scouting for "the next big thing".

Look out for specialist shows, such as the Dorset Chilli Festival, a less expensive option, where you could really sell a lot of your chilli concoction to knowledgeable chilli fans, chat about it with them, and make strong face-to-face connections with a potential fan-base already disposed to love your product.

At the big shows, such as The BBC Good Food Show, there are streams of people coming past you, and lots of other competing attractions.

But if you can be showcased within that show as a BBC Good Food Show bursary award winner, you may find that, like **Sarah Churchill of Artisan Kitchen**, founder of a preserves business made in a Gloucestershire kitchen, that the publicity leads on to great things. This year she was one of DEFRA's Food Stars and went to 10 Downing Street.

Social media

Katy Riddle was events manager for Deputy Prime Minister Nick Clegg, until in 2014 her passion for food took her in a new direction. She now runs Market Fresh Communications: a full service PR, digital marketing and event management consultancy for London food industry brands, including producers, chefs, restaurants and retailers.

Katy knows everything there is to know about getting a brand noticed on social media, and building food events. Here's her blueprint for how to do it effectively for your product, service and brand.

Social media platforms such as Facebook, Twitter, Instagram and Pinterest can be hugely powerful marketing tools for food businesses when used effectively.

The great news for start-ups with very limited advertising budgets is that these platforms are also practically free to run (provided you are willing to invest a little bit of time and energy)!

It'r also important to remember that most adults in the UK now use the internet for research and are registered users on at least one social media account – so it'o highly likely that your current and prospective customers are already talking about you on social media!

Like any marketing platform, an effective social media campaign for a food business should focus on:

- **Increasing awareness about the brand** and its products to the business target audiences (i.e. potential customers and opinion formers).

- **Building the branding positive reputation** and growing the business on supporter base.

In order to achieve these objectives, a successful social media campaign should focus on the following strategies:

- **Promoting** the brand through proactive posts highlighting the product(s), benefits of use and "story"/USP.

- **Engaging** directly with other users who the brand may appeal to (i.e. potential customers or opinion formers).

- **Collaborating** with complementary brands who can help the brand to achieve its objectives.

Top tips for effective social media use

Make sure that everything you post via your social media account is consistent with your brand't key messages, ethos and personality (your "voice").

Don't post anything on social media that you wouldn't say to someone in person (or want a potential customer to think about your brand)!

Regularly repeat your key messages – remember that your post is one of hundreds presented to your target social media users at any one time (and that not all of your followers will be online at the same time).

Don't worry that users will get "bored" with the same photo or reading about the key benefit of your product.

Remember that you can post the same piece of interesting content on each of your social media platforms, and even "reshare" one post across your other accounts/platforms to encourage users to follow you on multiple channels (e.g. post the link to your great Instagram photo on your Twitter profile and your Facebook page).

Think about the timing of your social media posts, to take advantage of the busiest periods (e.g. when people are commuting or relaxing in front of the TV in the evening), and times when your messages are most likely to appeal to your target audience (food products will always be more popular at meal times, when people are hungry!).

There are many social media management services that will allow you to schedule your posts to be published at a certain time (and are often free if you only have one brand).

Posts with either a website link or an image (or both) have been proven to result in the highest engagement from other social media users ("likes", comments and reshares).

Instagram is now the fastest growing social media platform – as people "eat with their eyes", and this is particularly good news for food businesses!

Instagram offers a number of excellent photo editing tools and filters – take advantage of these to improve the quality of your photos and develop a style of photo that suits your brand.

Instagram users love "behind the scenes" images – more good news for hands-on independent producers!

Post photos to provide your followers with an insight into your brand and background (e.g. in your product kitchen, visiting your suppliers/sourcing ingredients, delivering products to a new stockist, team photos at food shows), and taking into account anything confidential/any brand secrets not to show!

Include hashtags in your posts to allow your messages to reach more users. A hashtag is a word or phrase with the # sign before it, which makes it searchable (e.g. #shoplocal #followfriday)

Take advantage of popular hashtags, especially those relating to key benefits of your brand/product (e.g. #glutenfree #vegan).

Include one or two hashtags on Twitter and Facebook posts for the highest engagement, but include as many hashtags as relevant on Instagram posts.

Create special hashtags for social media competitions or events and encourage your followers to use these hashtags in their posts.

You can also track the "reach" of a particular hashtag to see how many users will have seen this.

Be careful when creating unique hashtags – if this is too niche or too difficult to read/understand then it isn't worth including as no-one else will be searching for it or using it (e.g. #artisanchocolatemadeincornwallusingclottedcream).

Search relevant hashtags to identify other social media users who your brand and product will appeal to (e.g. #vegan)

Proactively engage with these users by replying to/commenting on their posts, in order to introduce them to your brand and build a relationship

Take advantage of interesting content generated by other social media users and post this on your social media platforms too (e.g. recipes created by your customers using your product, or photos taken by your stockists showing your product on their shelves).

These posts demonstrate support for your brand from other users and therefore acts as an endorsement – this can be particularly useful if this other user is well known amongst your target audience or has a significant following.

Make sure to reply to the other user thanking them to help develop the relationship further, and credit them when re-sharing their post (a photo credit especially important).

Post interesting content from other sources that backs up your key messages (e.g. medical research on the benefits of an ingredient used in your product).

Post content from other users that complements your brand – this will help develop a collaborative relationship and hopefully encourage them to re-share your content too (e.g. details of a fun event hosted by one of your stockists that your customers may wish to attend).

Use competitions and prize draws to grow your brand following on a particular social media platform

Identify potential brand ambassadors/endorsers.

Run regular competitions and other exclusives (e.g. discounts, event invites, "first look" at new products) provide users with clear benefits to follow/engage with your social media accounts.

There are important legal rules/guidelines surrounding social media competitions, so read up on these beforehand and ensure that any promotion/offer you run complies with these (you can find the rules listed on the websites for the various social media platforms).

For more information on creating business accounts on social media platforms, visit:

Twitter for Business: https://business.twitter.com

Facebook for Business: www.facebook.com/business

Instagram for Business: https://business.instagram.com/

Pinterest for Business: https://business.pinterest.com/en

There are also many social media management services that you can use to publish your posts and track the growth in your social media profiles.

Here are a few of the most prominent – it's also worth signing up to their newsletters and visiting their blogs for regular updates on the latest social media trends and more top tips:

Sumall: https://sumall.com/

Simply Measured: http://simplymeasured.com/

Social Bro: www.socialbro.com/

Social Bakers: www.socialbakers.com

Hootsuite: https://hootsuite.com

Buffer: https://bufferapp.com

Hubspot: www.hubspot.com

So there you have it, a master plan to follow, and if you need more consultancy advice from Katy, tweet her at @KatyMarketFresh on Twitter.

Staff

"Whole Foods Market sampling is as much about keeping staff aware of who you are, and getting them involved in your brand, as it is about sampling to your customers"

Dan Shrimpton, founder of Peppersmith, explains further:

"The difference between selling and not selling is being well merchandised and being well stocked."

"If you are a pleasant customer to deal with, the stores will treat you better."

Subscription

A subscription business model gives you regular sales and allows you to manage your cash flow so that it evens out across the year and can be guaranteed more easily than the highs and lows of individual orders.

By building a mailing list with the fabulously free Mailchimp (see page 86) you can write one email and reach hundreds of buyers.

Subscription food's best poster child is **http://graze.com** (where, I might add, it's very hard to find the unsubscribe button once you are signed up...).

Cocoa Runners deliver a monthly, beautiful (tissue-paper wrapped, with bar tasting notes) pack of artisan chocolatier handmade bars originating in Vietnam, San Francisco, and Scunthorpe (glorious Duffy's Red Star).

Just as you think: "Maybe I'll unsubscribe...." there's another intriguing flat box through the letterbox, tempting you to unwrap its glories and savour the contents one more time.

You can send their single Discovery boxes to friends as gifts, and also "build your own gift box" from their bean to bar made by artisans chocolate library.

My lovely other half who bought me a subscription, says Cocoa Runners email him twice a week to prompt him to buy – and he does – he sends our trainee teacher daughter chocolate bars by post, to her delight.

Hello Fresh is a London-based meal ingredients delivery service, with everything weighed and measured for you to whip up a fresh tasty meal at home.

Their advice on how they have built sales of their high-end meal solution for busy people?

They leaflet Amazon customers inside their Amazon book deliveries (affluent, busy people) to raise awareness of Hello Fresh with a discounted offer on the first order.

They discount the first purchase online so people try them out.

They also send rather handsome guys to hand out Hello Fresh leaflets, with discounts on first order, during the evening rush hour at tube stations in posh bits of London.

Some customers only buy once, but with email address capture and then in-box access to those buyers, Hello Fresh's team say: "Email sign-ups allow us to remind customers to buy again".

Hello Fresh uses friendly phone calls to persuade/understand nearly-customers who don't buy.

Hello Fresh are attracting new customers across seven markets and have just raised £85m in their latest funding round from international investors.

Testing

From the moment you take a stand at a fair or at a market, you are testing your idea on strangers.

The most important bit of testing equipment you need to have with you?

Your mouth to ask questions. Your ears to hear the answers.

Which of your products, be they brownie flavours, or pickles or nut milks, do they immediately choose first?

What are they drawn to straight away, the minute they approach your products? If customers pick these products up, and buy, something is working just right. You need to find out what it is so you can do more of it.

There is *one* simple question that I use in all my food research projects for established brands in supermarkets. It's all you need to ask to find out so much useful stuff:

"What attracted your eye to that just now?"

You'll hear:

"It's the ingredients, such an interesting combination, I was intrigued..."

"It looks delicious, and I was planning melon and prosciutto for lunch...."

"My boyfriend loves chilli sauce and I was thinking of getting it for him...."

Equally, if your range or your marshmallows have some flavours that just don't sell very well, you need to know WHY. What's putting people off?

It could be the appearance of the product, how it looks, it could be fears about its spiciness, it could be an ingredient that is "love it or hate it", like beetroot. If you know what it is, you can fix it. So don't be afraid to listen hard.

Feedback, especially when negative, gives you things you can fix to convert more potential customers into actual spenders.

Trends

Trends move fast in London, then gradually ripple out to other parts of the UK.

That's why cupcakes are still big in Buckinghamshire, but for cutting-edge Londoners they're social death. It's either "raw", "sprouted", "cleanses" or the latest carbs category to be revitalised, doughnuts, in the former of Crosstown Doughnuts.

Appearing in a Piccadilly Circus tube pop-up, and now with daily deliveries to London's Whole Foods Market, Selfridges and a scattering of artisan coffee joints across the capital, Adam Wills (who co-founded Gourmet Burger Kitchen, a "better" burger joint) has re-vamped this nostalgic sugar covered delight.

Spearheading the doughnut renaissance, his flavours include Sea Salt Caramel and Banana, Crème Brulée, and my personal favourite, the Belgian Chocolate Truffle Doughnut, "dusted with bittersweet cocoa powder, and filled with a decadent milk chocolate truffle mousse". Bring on the better doughnut, I say, infinitely nicer than a Krispy Kreme.

The point of this story?

Make sure that your wheatgrass juice shots will work in Reading. Are they ready for birch water in Banbury? Are there enough customers who will buy you regularly? Have you found a detox café in Doncaster where you can be stocked and sell in quantity?

Innocent drinks' edamame beans in their veg pots did *not* impress Wakefield shoppers – "what the 'ell's this?"

Will your food idea work outside fashion-conscious London? And will folk tire of it and move on?

You need customers who buy every day.

Surf a trend, for sure, but make sure your idea can still swim on its own, when these food fashion waves have broken on the shore…

Twitter

Tweet what you are about and your story.

People can buy *any* drink or any snack.

If they feel personally connected to the founder of the business that makes what they eat or drink, that emotion keeps them coming back to you.

Twitter has a massive foodie community in the UK that is supportive, generous, interested, kind, intrigued by new products, experimental and shares like crazy!

A few minutes a day, first thing in the morning, tweeting and responding to and thanking followers is gold dust in terms of "the no cost but your time" attention it gets you and your product.

Take a look at innocent drinks' twitter timeline, or Daylesford (if you are a café/food event pop-up business) for a free master class in how to tweet with fun, beauty and humour and occasional mentions of your product. Then get creative in your own style!

On Twitter you can actively hunt for stockists such as delis and independent cafés and food shops who will stock you. Go after them! Nicely! Ditto distributors!

Unifying

Tips from the experts: unifying your range to increase sales

Simon Day, founder of unearthed, a world food brand,

offers the following advice on bringing your products together in-store to attract more attention. (NB: Most supermarkets won't let you do this, and keep you in their chosen categories, but you can try. Bear snacks got their product stocked alongside fresh produce, by the fruit. Give a persuasive argument an airing.)

Simon explains:

> "Our best example of unifying was what we call the 'unearthed bay'.

> We secured a full bay of space in Waitrose stores to bring together 40 products that we felt consumers would like to buy together and put them all together on the shelves on a two for £5 deal.

> Things such as olives and cured meats would have sat close together anyway (although not this close) but our Spanish Omelette and Tarte Flambée were examples of products that sat in a different part of store with quiches and the like, before we included them in this bay promotion.

> We also produced some excellent prawn skewers that brought some variety to the bay – after all, if you were eating tapas out of home you would probably want to order a mix of seafood, meat and vegetable dishes.

> The results were that sales of unearthed grew by over 20% year on year (in large part due to this initiative), redemption

levels on the promotion were much higher than we expected from previous promotions, our consumers are now buying more unearthed products per trip, and more over the year, and the bay stayed in longer than originally planned because Waitrose were very happy with its performance. When it is right for shoppers, then everyone gains!"

Vanity metrics

You know the kind of thing I mean, food businesses or people with thousands of likes on Facebook (probably bought from a "click-farm" in the Philippines).

The latest "health gurus" with whom you feel you can't compete for sociability, popularity, profile, and sheer "popping up everywhere"-ness.

The first rule of confidence?

Don't compare. Don't count your likes. Don't worry about how many followers you have.

As Richard Reed, co-founder of innocent drinks, says:

"A like is NOT a sale."

It's sales that matter. Keep them the main thing.

- Who is your next shop stockist?
- How can you get to new retail buyers?
- What sales proof do you need to convince the buyer?

These should be on your list of must-do's. Tackle them first.

How are your sales of products doing? Are they what they should be? If not, why not?

Can you do more to boost them? (See Powerful promotions, page 94 and Sampling, page 107).

Why does my product sell in some stores and not in others?

Stores vary enormously. They may look the same. They're not.

This sounds blindly obvious, but I'll say it anyway. Stores are situated in different neighbourhoods, with different sets of people shopping there. Neighbourhoods change.

A Budgens in Islington may stock and sell many more expensive foodie convenience items than a Budgens in West Ealing. A Waitrose that was formerly a Somerfield store does not magically go up-market because it has the badge of Waitrose.

A Sainsbury's in Balham may suddenly have big sales taking off in the yoghurt aisle because young families have just bought houses in the area and are feeding Yeo Valley to their kids every single day.

The Whole Foods Market behind Piccadilly Circus serves the young runners and researchers in the film industry in Soho, who are earning nothing. They are so much more price aware than the international bankers' wives shopping in Whole Foods Kensington.

I've seen many food companies be listed in their first 100 Waitrose stores, and find that the rate at which they sell products each week is dramatically higher in some of those stores than others.

Which leads to the tricky question: do you sample where your product isn't selling well to try to boost sales, or are you flogging a dead horse? Or do you concentrate your sampling where sales are already good, to increase them further? There's no easy answer to this, but Waitrose will demand a certain number of sales across all the stores you are stocked in, and your poor performers will drag down your good stores to an average across the board.

So if you can work out where and why your product has taken off, and with whom, you can then try to seek out those customers elsewhere and encourage them in other locations to buy you.

Look, listen, and learn when sampling, and you should spot some similarities in the customers you see that give you clues – do they like entertaining/are they young/old, are they male/female?

Always ask the store managers who shops in the store – they know their customers really well, and can help you understand the area.

X marks the spot

The very sweet spot.

The moment when your product sells regularly and steadily, every week, flying off those shelves.

If you've:

- made a good product
- priced it right
- sized it correctly
- packaged it appealingly
- got it in the right places where your target customers shop
- got them to notice it
- and to buy it repeatedly….

Bingo! You've hit your sweet spot. Congratulations!

Now, what are you going to make next to increase your sales? (See Innovation on page 76)

You

Are you working on your own? Self-employed? Solopreneur? Sole trader?

(By the way, someone needs to come up with sexier titles for us lovely people, please, rather than ones that sound like we're unlucky in love, or worse, "micro-business", which makes me feel like cress seeds grown amateurishly on a flannel.)

If it's all up to you, (or you and an intern), the secret of flourishing is *this*:

- switch off, take time out, work smarter, laugh, keep a perspective, and find buddies.

It's a 24:7 social media always available NIGHTMARE now – if you aren't on Instagram with your breakfast/selfie/latte at 7a.m., with artful filters, you're not in the game.

In the daytime you're sorting out orders, logistics, making the product and marketing. If you've got someone else making your product, you still have tons to do. If you run a bakery or café, you have staff to organise, customers to please. You're writing against deadlines, blogging for a book deal, recipe testing or styling it out, tweeting or Facebooking....

In the evening you're appearing at pop-up events in Shoreditch, baking round the clock, invoicing, and just generally worrying.

Switch off

We're always being told to switch off. And the secret is to actually *do* it.

Walk out briskly leaving your phone behind or turning it off. Just for 20 minutes. The world won't end. Feel the sun, and the air. Just breathe.

Get into whatever bit of nature you can, a park, a river, a square, where there might be things other than humans, such as trees and birds.

I scull on the Thames. An hour rowing up to Chiswick in a boat on my own, against the pressure of the tide, avoiding the buoys, and admiring the cormorants fishing, clears out my head like nothing else. It's a refreshing mini-holiday. Find out what your mini-vacation is. Take it.

Take time out

Dana Elemara, Founder of Arganic, and Amelia Rope, chocolatier, both take time to go to the Victoria & Albert Museum to be inspired. Make sure your weekends are proper weekends, or at least a half day or day off, if you can't take two.

Work smarter

As Richard Reed, co-founder of innocent drinks says, "Keep the main thing the main thing."

Is what you are doing each day moving the business towards your bigger sales goals, or are you just fire-fighting?

You could make a list of tiny easy things to do. Or you could think about how to get nearer to the bigger more important goal – where do you want to be sold next?

Is there an event you could speak at where you would reach three hundred people who are potential customers? (If you're a food business founder, chances are the *Guardian* Masterclasses on food might be interested in you telling your story.)

Could you appear on local radio?

Are you sampling regularly? Could you train an intern to represent your brand who can do some of the talking and sampling for you? And regain your time for more strategic, harder stuff?

Always link these goals to your end-game: getting more people to know about you, and achieving more sales.

Laugh!

I know when I've hit the wall – my sense of humour goes, I get cross easily, and I feel tetchy. My lovely daughter Flora will then invite me to the sofa for a half hour of comedy TV. The endorphins are great. Recommended!

Keep a perspective

It's so easy to become absolutely obsessed about your business. It's your baby. *Of course* you want to spend every waking moment on it. But there's a difference between working in your business and on your business. Stepping away is really important.

I know lots of food entrepreneurs who have got ill over-working. Balance is important: you're in this for the long haul.

Running a food business is a marathon, but weirdly, also has some fast sprints in there too. Be prepared and take care of yourself!

Zen habits

If you've got this far, well done. A big thank you for sticking with me.

I am now going to share with you one of the places on the internet that *is* worth spending time in.

Sign up for Zen Habits.

Leo Babuta's Zen Habits newsletter is the only newsletter I never delete.

Why?

Because he teaches you how to change your habits and *get stuff done*, without being preachy or dictatorial.

How to do less. Yet actually do more.

If you're running a food business, and increasing sales, building relationships with buyers, chasing cash flow and customers, explaining your product over and over, you need help to develop helpful structured daily habits.

My personal Zen Habit (thanks, Leo) "not leaving the room till it's done" helps me with super-hard tasks.

Like the sales call you should make, the pitch preparation for the buyer that you need to research, and most of all, calming yourself down in the face of competing demands, so you can work out which to do first.

Zest

I'm hoping some of the tips in this book have given you renewed zest for sharing your product or service, and made the selling seem easier. I wish you good luck with the selling!

All the best, come chat to me on Twitter @Tessa_Stuart

Tessa x

Acknowledgements

I'd like to thank all the kind food business founders who shared their time and advice so freely with me for this book.

In order of appearance in the pages:

Rekha Mehr www.linkedin.com/pub/rehka-mehr
@RekhaMehr

Maike Hachfeld – owner of Hack and Veldt
www.hackandveldt.com

Marcus Carter Artisan Food Club www.foodventures.co.uk

Ben O'Brien – founder of Sourced Market
www.sourcedmarket.com

Leah Anderson-O'Loughlin, former bakery and dairy buyer at Selfridges (now to be found in Melbourne, Australia)

Sarah Hilleary – founder of B-Tempted Gluten Free
@BTemptedHQ @sarahhilleary

Lucy Woodhouse – co-founder of Claudi & Fin
www.claudiandfin.co.uk

Amelia Harvey – co-founder of The Collective Dairy
www.thecollectivedairy.com/uk

Henrietta Morrison – founder of Lily's Kitchen
www.lilyskitchen.co.uk

Jim Cregan – co-founder of Jimmy's Iced Coffee
www.jimmysicedcoffee.com

Fergus Chamberlain – co-founder of Gran Luchito
www.granluchito.co.uk

innocent drinks www.innocentdrinks.co.uk

Camilla Barnard – co-founder of Rude Health
www.rudehealth.com

Paul Lindley – founder of Ella's Kitchen
www.ellaskitchen.co.uk

Rosie Millen aka Ms Nutritionist @ms_nutritionist

Amelia Rope – founder chocolatier www.ameliarope.com

@ameliarope

Escape The City – for City professionals longing to do
something meaningful www.escapethecity.org

@escthecity

The Guild Of Fine Food and Great Taste Awards
www.gff.co.uk

@guildoffinefood

Mark Campbell, Commercial Director of Higgidy
www.higgidy.co.uk

Tom Mercer – founder of MOMA! Foods
www.momafoods.co.uk

Lucy Wright and Anna Mackenzie – co-founders of Cuckoo
Foods www.cuckoofoods.co.uk

Charlotte Knight – founder of G'Nosh www.gnosh.co.uk

Dan Shrimpton – co-founder of Peppersmith
www.peppersmith.co.uk

Aideen Kirby – co-founder of Brew Tea
www.brewteacompany.co.uk

Katy Riddle – Director Founder of Market Fresh Comms
www.marketfreshcomms.com

Gill Foreshew – founder of The French Dressing Company
www.fdc-online.com

Asif Walli – co-founder of Duke Of Delhi
www.dukeofdelhi.com

Sarah Churchill – founder of Artisan Kitchen
www.theartisankitchen.co.uk

Cocoa Runners bean to bar chocolate subscription service
www.cocoarunners.com

Hello Fresh meal ingredients delivery www.hellofresh.co.uk

@hellofreshUK

Adam Wills – co-founder of Crosstown Doughnuts
www.crosstowndoughnuts.com

@CrosstownDough

Simon Day – founder of unearthed
www.discoverunearthed.com

@foodsunearthed

Lucy Thomas – founder of Tastemaker Ltd
www.tastemakerltd.co.uk @tastemakerltd